EQUITY AND FAIRNESS IN ISLAM

Mohammad Hashim Kamali

EQUITY AND FAIRNESS IN ISLAM

THE ISLAMIC TEXTS SOCIETY

This edition published 2005 by
The Islamic Texts Society
22a Brooklands Avenue,
Cambridge CB2 2DQ, UK

British Library Cataloguing-in-Publication Data
A catalogue record for this book is
available from the British Library

ISBN–13: 978-1-903682-41-8 *cloth*
ISBN–13: 978-1-903682-42-5 *paper*

ISBN–10: 1-903682-41-X *cloth*
ISBN–10: 1-903682-42-8 *paper*

ABOUT THE AUTHOR

Dr. Mohammad Hashim Kamali is Professor of Law at the International Islamic University of Malaysia, where he has been teaching Islamic law and jurisprudence since 1985. Born in Afghanistan in 1944, he studied law at Kabul University, where he was later appointed Assistant Professor. Following this he worked as Public Attorney with the Ministry of Justice in Afghanistan. He completed his LL.M. and his doctoral studies at London University, where he specialised in Islamic law and Middle Eastern Studies. Dr. Kamali then held the post of Assistant Professor at the Institute of Islamic Studies at McGill University in Montreal, and later worked as a Research Associate with the Social Science and Humanities Research Council of Canada. He is the author of *Law in Afghanistan: A Study of the Constitutions, Matrimonial Law and the Judiciary* (Leiden: E.J. Brill, 1985); *Principles of Islamic Jurisprudence* (third edition, Cambridge: The Islamic Texts Society, 2003); *Freedom of Expression in Islam* (Kuala Lumpur: Berita, 1994; new edition, Cambridge: The Islamic Texts Society, 1997); *Punishment in Islamic Law: an Enquiry into the Ḥudūd Bill of Kelantan* (Kuala Lumpur: Institute for Policy Research, 1995); *Freedom, Equality and Justice in Islam* (Cambridge: The Islamic Texts Society, 2002); *The Dignity of Man: An Islamic Perspective* (Cambridge: The Islamic Texts Society, 2002) and numerous articles in reputable international journals. He is twice recipient of the Ismāʿīl al-Fārūqī Award for Academic Excellence in 1995 and 1997.

Contents

PREFACE IX

PART ONE:

THE METHODOLOGY OF *ISTIḤSĀN* 1

INTRODUCTION 3

CHAPTER ONE: Meaning and Definition 11

CHAPTER TWO: Historical Perspective 17

CHAPTER THREE: *Istiḥsān*, *Maṣlaḥah* and Custom 24

CHAPTER FOUR: Types of *Istiḥsān* 29

CHAPTER FIVE: Proof (*ḥujjiyyah*) of *Istiḥsān* 58

CHAPTER SIX: The Argument Against *Istiḥsān* 63

CHAPTER SEVEN: *Istiḥsān* and Particularisation (*takhṣīṣ*) 71

CHAPTER EIGHT: A Review of the Methodology of *Istihsān* 75

PART TWO:

CONTEMPORARY APPLICATIONS 81

INTRODUCTION 83

CHAPTER NINE: The Issue of *Qabḍ* (taking possession) 85

CHAPTER TEN: Issues pertaining to *Awqāf* (charitable endowments) 92

Preface

Istiḥsān is the nearest Islamic legal doctrine to the western legal concept of equity. Both are essentially concerned with considerations of fairness and conscience, especially in cases which do not find a fair solution under the rules of positive law, that is, the law normally applied to such cases. This is because rules of law are usually formulated in an objective manner and style, and do not consider the peculiarities of particular cases and situations. The law may thus be applied to a case but the result may be less than satisfactory and fair. It is in such situations that *istiḥsān* in Islamic law, and equity in western jurisprudence, can play a role in order to find a fair solution to a particular problem.

This work is presented in two parts, one of which is devoted to the methodology of *istiḥsān*, and the other to its application to a select number of issues in the sphere of commercial transactions (*muʿāmalāt*). Part One is in turn subdivided into nine sections, each addressing a particular aspect of the methodology of *istiḥsān*. The introductory section draws attention to some of the unique features of *istiḥsān* when it is compared with other proofs of *Sharīʿah*, such as general consensus (*ijmāʿ*), analogical reasoning (*qiyās*), and considerations of public interest (*maṣlaḥah*). Section Two addresses the definition of *istiḥsān* from the perspectives of the Ḥanafī, Mālikī and Ḥanbalī schools respectively, and this is followed in Section Three by a brief account of the origins of *istiḥsān*, which are traced back to the era of the Companions and early ulama of the first two centuries of Islam. Section Four ascertains the common ground between *istiḥsān*, *maṣlaḥah* and custom, which is then followed by a discussion of the varieties of *istiḥsān* in the next section. Most of the examples and illustrations of *istiḥsān*, which occur in respect of a variety of themes, can be found in this section. The fairly large number of examples that I have given of *istiḥsān* is characteristic of this doctrine since it is basically concerned with particular cases and situations, rather than with laying down general principles and doctrines. The next three sections are each devoted to a discussion of the textual evidence of the Qur'ān and *Sunnah* in support of *istiḥsān*, the argument against *istiḥsān*, and the issue of the particularisation of the effective cause (*ᶜillah*) respectively. The main point addressed in this last section is whether *istiḥsān* is a form of particularisation of the *ᶜillah* of the ruling (*ḥukm*) for which it seeks to find an alternative. This point is then taken up again along with a general review of the methodology of *istiḥsān*, in Section Nine, which concludes the first part of this volume.

Part Two is an attempt at applying *istiḥsān* to certain issues of contemporary concern. These issues are related to sale, Islamic banking and charitable endowment (*waqf*), as well as the case of unclaimed assets in pension funds and other long-term saving accounts. A section is devoted to each of these issues, where I have reviewed the position in the existing *fiqh*, identified the issues, and then the alternative solution, if any, that could be obtained through the application of *istiḥsān*. The analysis of these issues and the possible solutions suggested for them are largely based on my own views, which are not devoid of a degree of speculation. This too is to some extent a characteristic feature of *istiḥsān*. Since *istiḥsān* mainly consists of a juristic opinion, any new solution that it offers is likely to partake of speculative effort, and its accuracy is likely to be tested by its acceptance or rejection over time. The concluding section addresses the relationship of *istiḥsān* to the goals and objectives of *Sharīᶜah*, the *maqāṣid al-Sharīᶜah*, and draws attention to its potential, and how it works as an instrument for securing the *maqāṣid*. The discussion here also highlights a certain lack of convergence between the science of *uṣūl al-fiqh* and the *maqāṣid al-Sharīᶜah*, and then explores the possibility of how *istiḥsān* could integrate the *uṣūl* and the *maqāṣid* into a broader and more coherent legal theory of the *Sharīᶜah*.

Mohammad Hashim Kamali
International Islamic University Malaysia
April 2003

PART ONE

THE METHODOLOGY OF *ISTIḤSĀN*

Introduction

Istiḥsān is primarily a juristic, not an economic, doctrine which can, however, be gainfully applied to economic issues of contemporary concern. The *ᶜulamā'* of jurisprudence have generally recognised certain limitations to the application of almost every one of the wide range of the recognised proofs of *Sharīᶜah*, with the exception of the Qur'ān, and *istiḥsān* is no exception. It is, however, interesting to note that *istiḥsān* is closely related to *qiyās* and *maṣlaḥah* as I have elaborated below, but while the *ᶜulamā'* of *uṣūl al-fiqh* (the science of the sources of law) have overruled the application of both *qiyās* and *maṣlaḥah* to devotional matters (*ᶜibādāt*), they have not suggested that the same restrictions be imposed on *istiḥsān*. As a principle of jurisprudence, *istiḥsān* applies to civil transactions (*muᶜāmalāt*) as well as *ᶜibādāt*; indeed the entire range of the *aḥkām*. This means that the scope of *istiḥsān* is wider than general consensus (*ijmāᶜ*) and analogical reasoning (*qiyās*), and also probably all the other subsidiary proofs. Our elaboration of the role and purpose of *istiḥsān* will presently show that *istiḥsān* applies to the rulings not only of *ijmāᶜ* and *qiyās* but also to the laws of the Qur'ān and *Sunnah*, although not in a normative sense. *Istiḥsān* applies to all of these proofs in the secondary capacity of ensuring that the strict application of the laws of *Sharīᶜah* does not go against their original purpose of attaining justice. It thus appears that *istihsān* is generic but not normative, and although it applies to the entire range of the *aḥkām*, its main purpose is to prevent irregularity in their application. The basic intent of *istiḥsān* is to ensure harmony between the letter and the spirit of the law, but its application is confined to cases and situations where a conflict arises between the letter and the spirit of *Sharīᶜah* due mainly to the factual peculiarities and circumstantial anomalies of particular cases.

The importance of *istiḥsān* as a harmoniser between the externality and intent of the *aḥkām* can be readily visualised when one is reminded that the *Sharīᶜah* is a legal system which is basically textual in that the highest proofs of *Sharīᶜah*, namely the Qur'ān and *Sunnah*, have been transmitted in finite texts which, however, have timeless validity and application. Without wishing to enter into detail, the Qur'ān and *Sunnah* are contained in finite texts, which are however, inherently dynamic when one bears in mind their emphasis on such values as justice, benevolence (*iḥsān*), the removal of hardship, and *maṣlaḥah*. But even so, the letter and text of the Qur'ān and *Sunnah* lay down a framework that is basically not changeable. The realities of life and the practicalities of transactions (*muᶜāmalāt*) have always been changeable with ever increasing rapidity. The jurist and *mujtahid* is thus faced with the task of injecting pragmatism into the fabric of the law, and, given the terms of this challenge, the need for a principle to ensure harmony between law and reality and between the letter of the law and its original purpose and spirit becomes immensely significant.

Like the other rational proofs of *uṣūl al-fiqh*, *istiḥsān* has often been studied in a scholastic and theoretical framework, and has not been utilised as a functional formula with which to find solutions to issues arising from the unfolding complexities of applying the laws of *Sharīᶜah* to new situations, which may be accompanied by conflicting interests and may therefore require a departure from the existing rules. *Istiḥsān* is after all a part of the broader concept of *ijtihād* and has suffered a similar decline to that of *ijtihād*. The present study is a modest attempt to analyse the methodology and dynamics of *istiḥsān* and then exploring its application to some issues of economic interest where it could be gainfully applied. But the scope and size of the challenge is such that sustained effort over a much longer period would be necessary to revitalise this particular area of *ijtihād*. It is well to remember that we live at the tail end of many long centuries of juristic stagnation and *taqlīd*, which makes it necessary to utilise the wider resources of *ijtihād* and to take the initiative, even at the risk of indulging in a measure of speculation and doubt, in order to relay the rich methodology of *uṣūl al-fiqh* and *ijtihād* to problems of contemporary concern. *Istiḥsān* can best relate to specific cases and issues within the framework of the existing legal status quo. It can address the irregularities, if any, of the existing law by suggesting necessary exceptions to its rules or providing alternative solutions where strict adherence to the existing law might fail to secure benefit and justice. *Istiḥsān* does not, on the whole, seek to introduce new rules and new legislation, but seeks to refine the existing law in relation to particular issues and circumstances. In this sense *istiḥsān* is basically circumstantial and piecemeal, and must develop in conjunction with issues as and when they arise. The substance of *istiḥsān* can thus be expected to emerge and materialise through a sustained and cumulative process that is aimed, in the true spirit of *ijtihād*, at injecting flexibility and pragmatism into the textual laws of the *Sharīʿah*, and ensuring internal consistency between the letter and the spirit of its rules.

Notwithstanding the measure of juristic technicality that seems to have been injected into this originally simple idea, *istiḥsān* remains basically flexible, and can be used for a variety of purposes, as we will discuss later. Yet because of its essential flexibility, the jurists have discouraged over-reliance on *istiḥsān*, lest it results in the suspension of the injunctions of *Sharīʿah* and becomes a means of circumventing its principles. *Istiḥsān* has thus become the subject of controversy among jurists. Whereas the Ḥanafī, Mālikī and Ḥanbalī jurists have considered *istiḥsān* a valid proof, the Shāfiʿī, Ẓāhirī and Shīʿī *ʿulamā'* have rejected it altogether and refused to give it any credibility in their formulation of the legal theory of the *uṣūl al-fiqh*.[1]

Enforcing existing law may prove to be detrimental in certain situations and a departure from it may be the only way of attaining a fair solution to a particular problem. The jurist who resorts to *istiḥsān* may find the law either too general, or too specific and inflexible. In both cases, *istiḥsān* may offer a means of avoiding hardship, and a solution harmonious with the higher objectives of the *Sharīʿah*. It has been suggested that the ruling of the second caliph, ʿUmar b. al-Khaṭṭāb, not to enforce the *ḥadd* penalty of the amputation of the hand for theft during a widespread famine, and the ban he imposed on the sale of the slave-mother (*umm al-walad*), and marriage with the *kitābiyahs* (mainly Christian and Jewish women) in certain cases, were all instances of *istiḥsān*. For the caliph set aside established law in these cases on grounds of public interest, equity and justice.

The Hanafī jurist, al-Sarakhsī (d. 483/1090), considered *istiḥsān* to be a method of seeking facility and ease in legal injunctions. It involves a departure from *qiyās* in favour of a ruling which repels hardship and brings about ease for the people. 'Removal of hardship (*rafʿ al-ḥaraj*)' al-Sarakhsī added, 'is a cardinal principle of religion which is enunciated in the Qur'ān'.[2] *Istiḥsān* is in perfect harmony with the substance of this message.

Al-Khuḍarī has rightly explained that in their search for solutions to problems, the Companions and Successors resorted to the Qur'ān and the normative example of the Prophet in the first place. But when they found no answer in these sources, they exercised their personal opinion (*ra'y*), which they formulated in light of the general principles and objectives of the *Sharīʿah*. This is illustrated, for example, in the judgement of ʿUmar ibn al-Khaṭṭāb in the case of Muḥammad ibn Maslamah. The caliph was approached by Maslamah's neighbour, al-Daḥḥāk b. al-Muzāḥim, who asked for permission to extend a water canal through Maslamah's property, and he was granted the request on the ground that no harm was likely to accrue to Maslamah, whereas extending the water canal was to the manifest benefit of his neighbour.[3] This was a departure from the normal rule pertaining to the integrity of the right of ownership, and the owner's privilege of whether to grant or turn down such a request.

It thus appears that *istiḥsān* is essentially a form of *ra'y* which gives preference to the best of the various solutions that may exist for a particular problem. In this sense, it is an integral part of Islamic jurisprudence and indeed of many other areas of human knowledge. Although the basic notion of *istiḥsān* in the sense of making necessary allowances and concessions in the strict application of normal rules can be found in the Qur'ān and *Sunnah*, as a juristic doctrine, *istiḥsān* could not be said to be a concern of either the Qur'ān or the *Sunnah*, simply because of the normative status of the Qur'ān and *Sunnah* as the most authoritative of all proofs. Juristic preference basically refers to the works of the jurists who attempt to reconcile the law with the exigencies of particular issues by suggesting exceptions and alternatives to the normal rules. The Qur'ān and *Sunnah* lay down the law, they make the normal rules, so to speak, and any exception or concession that is granted therein also becomes normative and is no longer a matter of juristic preference.

Evidence suggests that the Companions and Successors were not literalists who would seek a specific authority in the revealed sources for every legal opinion (*fatwā*) they issued. On the contrary, their rulings were often based on their understanding of the general spirit and purpose of the *Sharīʿah*, and not necessarily on the narrow and literal meaning of its principles. *Istiḥsān* has been formulated in this spirit; it is the antidote of literalism and it takes a broad view of the law, which must serve, not frustrate, the ideals of fairness and justice.

To give an example, oral testimony is the standard form of evidence in Islamic law on which a general consensus (*ijmāᶜ*) can be claimed to exist. Muslim jurists have insisted on oral testimony and have given it priority over other methods of proof, including confession and documentary evidence. In their view, the direct and personal testimony of a witness who speaks before the judge with no intermediary in between is the most reliable means of discovering truth. The question arises, however, of whether one should still insist on oral testimony at a time when other methods such as photography, sound recording, laboratory analyses, etc. offer at least equally, if not more, reliable methods of establishing facts. Here we have, I think, a case for recourse to *istiḥsān* which would give preference to these new and more reliable means of proof. It would mean departing from an established rule of evidence in favour of an alternative ruling which is justified in light of new circumstances. The rationale of this *istiḥsān* would be that the law requires evidence in order to establish the truth, and not oral testimony for its own sake. If this is the real spirit of the law, then recourse to *istiḥsān* would seem to offer a better way of upholding that spirit.

The *mujtahid* (one who is qualified to carry out *ijtihād*) may resort to *istiḥsān* when he or she finds that a particular issue being investigated normally falls within the ambit of analogy (*qiyās*), a general text or a legal maxim of *fiqh*. However, applying the normal rules to the issue at hand proves to be less than satisfactory, and this in turn leads the *mujtahid* to the conclusion that the same issue could be otherwise determined by recourse to other evidences, such as textual injunction (*naṣṣ*), general consensus, necessity, *maṣlaḥah* or custom. The *mujtahid* is convinced that the proposed alternative, although at variance with the normal rules, is nevertheless preferable, simply because it provides a desired solution that is also harmonious with the goals and objectives of *Sharīᶜah*.

Recourse may also be had to *istiḥsān* when the *mujtahid* finds that a particular issue is not regulated by the established rules of *Sharīᶜah*, that is, when the law is totally silent with regard to it, and no ruling can be found in the *nuṣūṣ* or *ijmāᶜ*, but where two conflicting rulings can be obtained when the issue is referred to *qiyās*, one of which is an obvious analogy (*qiyās jalī*) with a readily detectable effective cause (*ᶜillah*) that comes to mind first, and the other is a more subtle analogy (*qiyās khafī*) whose relevance to the issue at hand is established upon further scrutiny and reflection. The latter solution is preferable since it is not a cursory solution, based on superficial resemblance, but one which is confirmed upon deeper consideration and analysis. The ruling so arrived at is a ruling of *istiḥsān* which consists of a departure from *qiyās jalī* to the more subtle *qiyās khafī*. The first of these two types of *istiḥsān* involves making an exception to a normal rule of *Sharīᶜah* which is why it is known as exceptional *istiḥsān* (*istiḥsān istithnā'ī*), and the second type is based on analogy (*qiyās*), which is why it is known as analogical *istiḥsān* (*istiḥsān qiyāsī*). The basic purpose of constructing *istiḥsān*, of both these types, is to obtain a better and more equitable solution to an issue.

Notwithstanding the fact that the *ᶜulamā'* of the various *madhāhib* have defined *istiḥsān* somewhat differently from one another, the basic notion of the departure of the *mujtahid* from one ruling to another and his preference for the latter, whether based on a particular evidence in the other recognised proofs of *Sharīᶜah* or preferring one *qiyās* to another *qiyās*, lies at the root of *istiḥsān* in all its varieties. The departure in question is known as *istiḥsān*, or a preferable departure, because of the stronger evidence that is found in its support. To act on the stronger of two evidences is the hallmark of *istiḥsān* and a central feature of its various definitions, as we will discuss below.

Istiḥsān is the nearest Islamic legal doctrine to the notion of equity in western jurisprudence, but the subject calls for some explanation. This is because *istiḥsān* and equity are similar but not identical. Equity is a Western legal concept grounded in the idea of fairness and conscience, and derives legitimacy from belief in natural rights or justice beyond positive law.[4] *Istiḥsān* in Islamic law and equity in Western law are both inspired by fairness and conscience, and both authorise departure from a rule of positive law when its enforcement leads to unfair results. The main difference between them is in the overall reliance of equity on the concept of natural law, and of *istiḥsān* on the values and principles of the *Sharīᶜah*. But this difference need not be over-emphasised if one bears in mind the convergence of values between the *Sharīᶜah* and natural law. Notwithstanding their different approaches to the question of right and wrong, for example, the values upheld by natural law and the divine law of Islam are substantially concurrent. Briefly, both assume that right and wrong are not a matter of relative convenience for the individual but derive from an eternally valid standard that is ultimately independent of human cognizance and adherence. But natural law differs from divine law in its assumption that right and wrong are inherent in nature.[5] From an Islamic perspective, right and wrong are determined not by reference to the nature of things, but because God has determined them as such. The *Sharīᶜah* is an embodiment of the will of God, the Lord of the universe and the supreme arbiter of values. If equity is defined as a law of nature superior to all other legal rules, written or otherwise, then this is obviously not what is meant by *istiḥsān*. For *istiḥsān* does not recognise the superiority of any other law over divine revelation, and the solutions it offers are for the most part based on principles upheld by divine law. Unlike equity, which is founded on the recognition of a superior law, *istiḥsān* does not seek to constitute an independent authority beyond the *Sharīᶜah*. *Istiḥsān*, in other words, is an integral part of the *Sharīᶜah* and it differs with equity in that the latter recognises a natural law apart from, and essentially superior to, positive law.[6] The emphasis of *istiḥsān* is, however, on the ends and objectives of the *Sharīᶜah*, as opposed to analogy (*qiyās*), which is basically letter-bound and relies on specific textual rulings. Thus when a ruling of *qiyās* fails to comply with considerations of equity and fairness, or proves to inflict rigidity and hardship, *istiḥsān* is invoked in order to find a more equitable solution that is harmonious with the purpose and spirit of the *Sharīᶜah*, even at the expense of departure from its specific rules.

Western commentators have generally rejected the idea of drawing a parallel between equity and *istiḥsān*. John Makdisi has discussed, in this connection, the views of R. Paret, Joseph Schacht, Chafik Chehata and Emile Tyan and has found some weaknesses in them. Paret and Schacht thought that since *istiḥsān* is strictly controlled within the bounds of the Qur'ān and *Sunnah*, it is therefore very different from the notion of equity in western law. Chehata commented that since Islamic law does not accept the notion of natural law, it could not accommodate the doctrine of equity. Without wishing to engage in technicalities, the main issue seems to be whether it is acceptable to subjugate equity, which is above the law, to a level at which it is controlled by the law. Western law allows this subjugation whereas Islamic law does not, and *istiḥsān* in the latter context is clearly controlled by the general objectives of the *Sharīᶜah*. It is equally true that *istiḥsān* entails a departure from textual and analogy-based rulings in favour of alternative solutions deemed to be more satisfactory and equitable. The end results of *istiḥsān* and equity may not be very different from one another, but the method and procedure by which they are obtained may differ in the two legal systems.[7]

NOTES

1. Cf. Al-Ṣābūnī, *et al.*, *al-Madkhal al-Fiqhī wa Tārīkh al-Tashrīᶜ al-Islāmī*, Cairo, Maktabah Wahbah, 1402/1982, p. 119f.
2. Sarakhsī, *Al-Mabsūṭ*. Beirut, Dār al-Maᶜrifah, 1406/1986, X, 145.
3. Khuḍarī, *Tā'rīkh al-Tashrīᶜ al-Islāmī*. 7th edn. Beirut: Dār al-Fikr, 1401/1981, p. 199.
4. Osborn, *Concise Law Dictionary*, 5th edition, London, Sweet and Maxwell, 1964, p. 124.
5. Cf. Kerr, *Islamic Reform*, Berkeley, University of California Press, 1961, p. 57.
6. Cf. Makdisi, 'Legal Logic and Equity in Islamic Law', *American Journal of Comparative Law*, 33 (1985), p. 90.
7. See for details Makdisi's article 'Legal Logic and Equity in Islamic Law'.

CHAPTER ONE

Meaning and Definition

Being a derivation of the root word *ḥasana*, *istiḥsān* literally means considering something good, preferable and beautiful. The reference is to beauty in its common sense, that which appeals to the eye and attracts the heart. The word can be used in an objective sense, or purely subjectively when, for example, a person, whether layman or jurist, likes something and considers it beautiful even if other people might think otherwise. The word is also used in reference to things which might be visible and obvious as well as those that are intellectually perceived.[1]

The juridical meaning of *istiḥsān* reflects its literal meaning in that the term refers to juristic preference, exercised by a qualified jurist and *mujtahid*, consisting of departure from an existing rule or principle of the law in a particular case, in favour of a different ruling that is considered preferable. The preference so exercised is prompted by the desire to search for a more equitable solution because of the rigidity and unfairness that is brought about by strict adherence to existing law, as explained earlier. Several definitions can be found for *istiḥsān* and they are not identical, each imparting some insight into the various approaches that the *ʿulamāʾ* have taken to the doctrine. The Ḥanafī jurist Abū'l-Ḥasan al-Karkhī (d. 340 AH) defined *istiḥsān* as follows:

> *Istiḥsan* is to depart from the existing precedent, by taking a decision in a certain case different from that on which similar cases have been decided, for a reason stronger than the one that is obtained in those cases.[2]

According to this definition, *istiḥsān* effectively means detaching a case from those comparable to it. Hence it is the reverse of *qiyās* in that *qiyās* actually means attaching or joining a case to those that are similar to it. It thus appears that *qiyās* and *istiḥsān* take two different approaches and they are in a basic sense the opposite of one another.

Abū Bakr al-Jaṣṣāṣ (d. 370 AH) defined *istiḥsān* as departure from a ruling of *qiyās* in favour of another ruling which is considered preferable.[3]

Abū'l-Ḥusayn al-Baṣrī (d. 436 AH) defined *istiḥsān* as 'abandoning one facet of *ijtihād* for another, the latter being the stronger of the two and it consists of fresh evidence which is not found in the former.'[4]

While quoting al-Karkhī's definition, al-Sarakhsī added: the precedent that is set aside by *istiḥsān* normally consists of an established analogy which may be abandoned in favour of a superior proof, namely the Qur'ān, *Sunnah*, necessity (*ḍarūrah*) or a stronger *qiyās*. Al-Sarakhsī himself defined *istiḥsān* as 'abandonment of an opinion to which *qiyās* would lead in favour of a different opinion supported by stronger evidence and adapted to what is convenient to the people'. He explained this further by saying that *istiḥsān* is: (a) to seek ease and convenience in legal injunctions; (b) to adopt what is accommodating and lenient; and (c) to take to tolerance and seek that which brings comfort. Al-Sarakhsī then quoted the Qur'ānic verse (al-Baqarah, 2:185) which declares ease and the removal of hardship to be the main intent and purpose of divine injunctions.[5]

Some Ḥanafīs have also defined *istiḥsān* as 'an indication (*dalīl*) arising in the mind of the *mujtahid*, which he cannot express or articulate in words.' The reference here is to the intuitive insight of the *mujtahid*: something 'sparks in the soul of the interpreter', as Maḥmassānī wrote, 'which he finds himself unable to express by words or to bring out by other means'.[6] This last definition is evidently focused on the personal conviction of *mujtahid*, but may also make reference to the difficulty involved in making out a case for it. Be that as it may, what is said here is not really a definition but one aspect of the basic idea of *istiḥsān*, which is why it has been criticised by many *ʿulamā'* including al-Ghazālī, al-Shāṭibī, Ibn al-Ḥājib, al-Taftāzānī and others.[7] Thus according to al-Ghazālī, when an idea cannot be demonstrated in words, it may be said to be no more than a part of the imagination. It must be verified by valid evidence whether or not it is legitimate.[8] Al-Shāṭibī has addressed the question of objectivity in the precedent of Companions and the fact that they have frequently resorted to their own *ijtihād* in matters on which no textual ruling could be found. But the decisions they arrived at were made in the light of the principles of *Sharīᶜah* and the manner in which they understood it. None of the Companions have 'ever said that I rule in this or that issue according to my personal inclination, or that it is based on what is dear to me and what I desire.' If any of them had become so totally subjective, they would have certainly provoked denunciation and criticism. The Companions were certainly aware of the demand for objectivity, as one finds in the Qur'ān in such pronouncements as 'We revealed to you the Book with the truth so that you judge among people by what God has shown to you.' (al-Nisā', 4:105) The demand for objectivity in the criteria on which judgement is based, adds al-Shāṭibī, is also evident in the teachings of *Sunnah* which the Companions undoubtedly observed.[9]

The Ḥanbalī definition of *istiḥsān* seeks to relate it more closely to the Qur'ān and *Sunnah*. Thus according to Ibn Taymiyyah (and also Ibn Qudāmah al-Maqdisī) '*istiḥsān* is the abandonment of one legal ruling for another which is considered better on the basis of the Qur'ān, *Sunnah* or consensus.'[10]

Notwithstanding the fact that the Mālikī jurists laid greater emphasis on *istiṣlāḥ* (consideration of public interest), they have nevertheless validated *istiḥsān*. The Mālikīs view *istiḥsān* as a broad doctrine which is less stringently confined to the Qur'ān and *Sunnah* than the Ḥanafīs and Ḥanbalīs have viewed it. Thus according to Ibn al-ᶜArabī, '*istiḥsān* is to abandon exceptionally what is required by the law because applying the existing law would lead to a departure from some of its own objectives.' For Ibn al-ᶜArabī the essence of *istiḥsān* was to act on 'the stronger of two indications—*aqwa al-dalilayn*.'[11] Ibn al-ᶜArabī elaborated that the departure in question may be justified by custom, *maṣlaḥah* or *ijmāᶜ*. To this al-Shāṭibī added that Imām Mālik and Abū Ḥanīfah saw this process as particularisation of the general on the basis of stronger evidence which is either obvious or implied. Imām Mālik was inclined to use *istiḥsān* on the basis of *maṣlaḥah*, whereas Abū Ḥanīfah would specify the general by reference to the saying of a Companion, especially when it was contrary to *qiyās*.[12] It has further been observed that the preference given to the stronger of the two evidences in the Mālikī definition actually means giving preference to a particular *maṣlaḥah* (*maṣlaḥah juz'iyyah*) over the general ruling of *qiyās*.[13] *Qiyās* here means both a ruling that is based on analogy and also a normal principle or ruling of existing law.

It thus appears that departure from an existing precedent on the ground of a more compelling reason is a feature of *istiḥsān* common to all the definitions reviewed above. This departure may be from an obvious *qiyās* to a more subtle or hidden *qiyās*, or it may consist of making an exception to a general rule of existing law. The jurist who attempts *istiḥsān* must be convinced of the essential merit of the departure from, or exception to, existing law and rely on specific evidence. The evidence in question may be a textual ruling, general consensus, necessity, public interest or custom, or indeed any valid evidence that is persuasive enough to convince the *mujtahid* that there is a case for *istiḥsān*.

Many writers who have discussed the various definitions of *istiḥsān* have found al-Karkhī's definition to be the most comprehensive. Upon closer examination, however, one may find a certain degree of ambiguity in all the definitions. The relative strength of the two rulings involved, for instance, may not be very obvious. But even so, the basic notion of *istiḥsān* is fairly clearly conveyed in its existing definitions. I personally find Ibn al-ᶜArabī's definition to be simpler yet inherently dynamic. Yet the more challenging aspect of *istiḥsān* is not so much the theoretical understanding of its idea and concept as its application to particular issues. It is equally true, however, that a clear understanding of the concept and methodology of *istiḥsān* must precede its application. The main focus of this presentation is to provide a fairly in-depth analysis of *istiḥsān* which is not confined to a theoretical exposition of the doctrine but one which brings the theoretical understanding of this important branch of *ijtihād* a step closer to reality. *Istiḥsān* can thus be seen as a functional formula to be utilised and applied in the search for appropriate solutions to certain issues.

Some commentators have seen *istiḥsān* as a principle of marginal significance, which cannot claim an independent status among the proofs that are delianeated in the conventional expositions of *uṣūl al-fiqh*: Since *istiḥsān* is generally described as acting upon the stronger of two rulings, and then the departure that is made from one evidence in favour of another is normally from one recognised proof to another recognised proof, it is concluded that *istiḥsān* is not a proof in its own right. In this regard, al-Shawkānī has stated that there is no basis for identifying *istiḥsān* as an independent proof, for if it relies on other proofs then it is basically repetitive, and if it is outside this framework, it is not a part of the *Sharīᶜah*. Whether it consists of a departure from one *qiyās* to another *qiyās* or from a general principle to a particular evidence, *istiḥsān* merely involves giving preference to one proof or evidence over another and in doing so, derives its basic justification from the *nuṣūṣ*, general consensus, *maṣlaḥah* and custom, and does not, as it were, create anything in its own name.

Notwithstanding some reservation that the present writer has about the substance of this characterisation, what has been said need not be seen as a point of weakness, for it can also be seen as a point of strength in that *istiḥsān* is shown to be integral and generic to the entire spectrum of the recognised proofs; it has a firm footing in other proofs and has a sound evidential basis. It might be a more accurate reflection on *istiḥsān* to say perhaps that as a methodology and formula it is more dominantly procedural than substantive. But even this may not do justice to the essence of *istiḥsān*, especially when it is admitted, as I elaborate below, that *istiḥsān* operates on the basis of an independent effective cause (*ᶜillah*), and does not merely function as a specifier of the *ᶜillah* of an existing *qiyās*.

In responding to the critics of *istiḥsān*, al-Sarakhsī seems to have visualised the evidential strength of *istiḥsān* when he observed: some people have disapproved of *istiḥsān* and considered it invalid. If their disapproval is merely of words and the manner of expression of a certain concept, then there is no objection to using whatever name they may choose for *istiḥsān*, but if they disapprove of the basic concept and idea of *istiḥsān*, then this is unacceptable. For one only departs from the normal rules and those of *qiyās jalī* to another ruling when this is warranted by the recognised proofs of *Sharīᶜah* and one acts upon the ruling of *istiḥsān* only when it relies on an evidence stronger than *qiyās jalī*.[14]

In his characterisation of *istiḥsān*, al-Shāṭibī concurred with Ibn al-ᶜArabī's analysis that *istiḥsān* is acting on the stronger of two proofs. Al-Shāṭibī also wrote that the Mālikī view of *istiḥsān* concurs with the analysis that it is not outside the sphere of the recognised proofs, even though *istiḥsān* also involves consideration of the consequences of acts (*ma'ālāt al-afᶜāl*), something that may or may not be considered in its underlying evidence, such as *qiyās*. If one were to ignore this factor, then perhaps *istiḥsān* consists of no more than telling us that applying this or that proof is good and preferable in a particular case, and that as such it does not propose a new methodology or proof in its own right.[15]

NOTES

1. Cf. Zaydān, *Al-Wajīz fī Uṣūl al-Fiqh*, Baghdad, Maktabah al-Quds, 1396/1976, p. 230; Mīqā, *Al-Ra'y wa Atharuh fī Madrasah al-Madīnah*, Beirut, Mu'assasah al-Risāla, 1405/1985, p. 396; al-Mikādi, 'Baḥth fī'l-Istiḥsān', in *Al-Majlis al-Aᶜla li-Riᶜāyat al-Funun wa'l-Adab wa'l-ᶜUlūm al-Ijtimaᶜiyyah*, Usbuᶜ al-Fiqh al-Islāmī, Damascus, 1380/1961, p. 343.

2. Al-Taftāzānī, *Sharḥ al-Talwīḥ ᶜala'l-Tawḍīḥ*, Beirut, Dār al-Kutub al-ᶜIlmiyyah, n.d., II, 81; Sarakhsī, *Mabsūṭ*, X, 145; Ḥasan, 'Analogical Reasoning' in *Islamic Jurisprudence*, Islamabad, Islamic Research Institute, 1986, p. 410.

3. Quoted by Abū Sulaymān, *Al-Fikr al-Uṣūlī*, 2nd edition, Jeddah, Dār al-Sharq, 1404/1984, p. 153 from the unpublished ms of *Al-Fuṣūl fī Tartīb al-Uṣūl*; see also Ḥasan, 'Analogical Reasoning', p. 410.

4 Taftāzānī, *Talwīḥ*, II, 81; Abū Sulaymān, *Al-Fikr al-Uṣūlī*, p. 153.

5. Sarakshī, *Al-Mabsūṭ*, X, 145; Ḥasan, 'Analogical Reasoning', p. 411; Kassim, 'Sarakhsī's Doctrine of Juristic Preference (Istiḥsān) as a Methodological Approach towards Worldly Affairs (*Aḥkām al-Dunyā*)' in *American Journal of Islamic Social Sciences*, 5 (1988), p. 186.

6. Mahmassānī, *Falsafah al-Tashrīᶜ fī'l-Islām: The Philosophy of Jurisprudence in Islam*. Trans. Farhat J. Ziadeh. Leiden: E.J. Brill, 1961, p. 85.

7. Cf. Taftāzānī, *Talwīḥ*, II, 82.

8. Al-Ghazālī, *Mustaṣfā min ᶜilm al-Uṣūl*, Cairo, al-Maktabah al-Tijāniyyah, 1356/1937, p. 281.

9. Al-Shāṭibī, *al-Iᶜtiṣām*, Cairo, Maṭbaᶜah al-Manār, 1332/1914, II, 150ff.

10. Ibn Taymiyyah, *Mas'alah al-Istiḥsān*, in John Makdisi (ed.), *Arabic and Islamic Studies in Honour of H.A.R. Gibb*, Cambridge (MA), Harvard University Press, 1965, p. 446.

11. Cf. Al-Shāṭibī, *Muwāfaqāt fī Uṣūl al-Sharīᶜah*, Cairo, al-Maktabah al-Tijāniyyah al-Kubrā, n.d., IV, 208.

12. Ibid., IV, 209.

13. Ibid., IV, 208.

14. Al-Sarakhsī, *Al-Mabsūṭ*, X, 145; Mīqā, *Al-Ra'y*, pp. 407-408.

15. Al-Shāṭibī, *Muwāfaqāt*, IV, 208.

CHAPTER TWO

Historical Perspective

The origins of *istiḥsān* can clearly be traced back to the Companions, especially the decision of the Caliph ʿUmar al-Khaṭṭāb to postpone the prescribed punishment of theft during the year of the famine on the ground that applying the normal rules under such conditions would fail to obtain justice and may even amount to oppression. The Caliph is also on record as having made two different decisions concerning a case of inheritance, known as *al-mushtarakah* (discussed below), the second of which set aside the normal rules of inheritance and provided a solution that seemed equitable and just under the circumstances.[1] The facts of these decisions leave little doubt as to the historical origins of *istiḥsān*, and yet one often reads in many a reputable text of *uṣūl al-fiqh* the attribution of *istiḥsān* to Imam Abū Ḥanīfah and his disciple al-Shaybānī. This is mainly because in *uṣūl al-fiqh*, *istiḥsān* is identified as a proof of law, and a technical doctrine of jurisprudence. The question is often posed as to the actual use of *istiḥsān* as a technical term and doctrine, and it is in this context that the juridical origins of *istiḥsān* are traced back only to Imam Abū Ḥanīfah and his contemporaries and disciples. Although ʿUmar al-Khaṭṭāb actually exercised the basic notion and idea of *istiḥsān*, he probably did not use the term, or in fact identify what he had done as a proof or principle of *uṣūl al-fiqh*.

The word *istiḥsān* appears to have been used, even before Imam Abū Ḥanīfah, by an early jurist and judge of the Umayyad period, Iyās b. Muʿāwiyah (d. 122/740). He is on record as having given the following instructions: 'Use *qiyās* as a basis of judgement so far as it is beneficial to the people, but when it leads to undesirable results then use juristic preference (*fa'staḥsinū*).'[2] This clearly indicates that even before Abū Ḥanīfah, *istiḥsān* was known as a principle by which to correct the irregularities of *qiyās*. Al-Qarāfī, who quoted Iyās's statement also posed the question: If this is the case, why was the exercise in question called '*istiḥsān*', and not called a *dalīl* (*evidence*) in its normative and original sense? The answer given is that *istiḥsān* is valid evidence, and the fact that it bears this name is due largely to technical reasons. Experts in the field have evidently recognised its significance by giving the formula a different name—and not merely subsuming it under the existing proofs. Essentially, *istiḥsān* signifies 'that which is good and valid in *Sharīᶜah*' and stands in harmony with it.[3] It also seems that early juristic practice had little difficulty in accepting *istiḥsān* and that *istiḥsān* became controversial only after Imam Abū Ḥanīfah, who has said on occasion that '*qiyās* is such and such but we apply *istiḥsān*,' often without elaborating on the underlying reasons for the decisions that were based on *istiḥsān*.[4] The Imam is also known, on the other hand, to have made such statements as 'had it not been for precedent (*athar*), I would have decided this case according to *qiyās*,' or 'had it not been in deference to *riwāyah* (transmitted ḥadīth) I would have decided the case by *qiyās*.' The Imam used to rely on *qiyās*, but when it led to an unsatisfactory result in a particular case, he resorted to *istiḥsān*, which meant turning away from *qiyās*. His disciple Muḥammad Ibn Ḥasan al-Shaybānī noted that 'when Abū Ḥanīfah exercised *qiyās*, his disciples used to argue with him, but when he resorted to *istiḥsān*, they did not argue as much.'[5] Statements like these suggest that the Imam used to rely on the authority of ḥadīth from the Prophet or approved precedent which might not have been generally known.[6] Failing these, he resorted to *qiyās*, and eventually to *istiḥsān* as an escape from the difficulties of *qiyās*. The fact that Imam Abū Ḥanīfah and other jurists of that period have not elaborated on the underlying reasons for their *istiḥsān*-oriented decisions and did not specify a particular procedure for *istiḥsān* provoked criticism from the Ahl al-Ḥadīth traditionists who charged the proponents of *istiḥsān* with arbitrariness and adjudication without textual evidence. One can only assume that the early jurists did not feel an urgent need to expound the evidential bases of their decisions that were based on *istiḥsān*. This is partly why it became difficult to distinguish the respective uses of *qiyās* and *istiḥsān* in the early period. The jurists of the pre-Shāfiᶜī period had still not provided a precise definition or methodological guidelines for *istiḥsān*. This had a particular bearing on the relationship of *istiḥsān* to *qiyās*, which has remained, as I shall later elaborate, somewhat controversial ever since.

Ibn al-Muqaffa' (d. 137/756), a state secretary of the early Abbasid period, observed that discretion cannot be precluded in the adjudication of matters not regulated in the textual sources. To attain justice and fairness in accordance with the spirit of the Qur'ān and *Sunnah*, it is necessary to exercise discretion, and he declared that unreserved adherence to *qiyās* sometimes leads to injustice, and it is in such instances that a certain degree of flexibility is advisable: '*Qiyās* is only an evidence that should be applied for good results(...) but when it leads to unfairness and injustice, one must not hesitate to abandon it. For the objective of the law is not adherence to *qiyās* as such, but to judge according to what is good and appropriate.'[7]

Abū Yūsuf (d. 182 AH) and al-Shaybānī (d. 189 AH) have utilised *istiḥsān* as a method by which to rectify the irregularities of *qiyās*. The purpose was not to deny the legitimacy of *qiyās* or to compromise its validity as a proof, but to restrict its scope so as to avoid unfavourable consequences that followed its rigid application. Al-Shaybānī has resorted to *istiḥsān* on the basis of custom, and abandoned *qiyās* when it went against what was accepted by valid custom. He said, for example, that if the inhabitants of a town or a fort seek the protection of the Muslim forces and it is granted to them, the protection according to *qiyās* would only be extended to the town or the fort but not to their contents. By recourse to *istiḥsān*, however, the protection so granted would also cover their contents. For the customary understanding of words *qal'ah* and *madīnah* (fort and town) do not simply refer to a physical environment and buildings but also to their contents and inhabitants.[8]

Al-Shaybānī also resorted to *istiḥsān* on the basis of exigencies that entailed a departure from the ruling of ḥadīth. For instance, the ḥadīth which proscribes the sale of non-existing objects at the time of contract invalidates the advance sale of manufactured goods (i.e. *istiṣnā'*). Al-Shaybānī, however, held that *istiṣnā'* was valid because of its necessity, despite it being contrary to the ruling of the ḥadīth.[9]

Abū Yūsuf exercised *istiḥsān* when he held that the husband of a woman who renounced Islam and became an apostate in her terminal sickness (*maraḍ al-maut*) was entitled to inherit from her. The normal rules of *Sharī'ah* do not permit inheritance between Muslims and non-Muslims, which is why under normal circumstances the husband would not qualify to inherit from his deceased wife if she had renounced Islam. However, Abū Yūsuf held that the husband is entitled, by way of *istiḥsān*, to inherit from his deceased wife, and explained that it was just possible that the woman's apostasy during her mortal illness was a matter of malice in order to nullify the husband's right to inheritance. The ruling of *istiḥsān* is thus preferred here because *qiyās* does not make a provision to differentiate between the two states of normal illness and mortal illness (*maraḍ al-maut*), and it is through *istiḥsān* that a different ruling can be provided for the latter.[10]

On a similar note, if someone employs a labourer to dig a well in the vicinity of a public path, the employer must obtain advance permission from the ruler. Supposing that this was done and a well was excavated, and then someone fell into the well and died as a result, the labourer, according to *qiyās*, would be held responsible. Abū Yūsuf on the other hand held that *qiyās* should be abandoned because the labourer had acted under instruction of an employer who had also obtained the ruler's permission. By recourse to *istiḥsān*, Abū Yūsuf held the employer's family and kin (*ʿāqilah*) responsible for the payment of blood money (*diyyah*) in compensation.[11]

Imam Mālik's (d. 179 AH) understanding of *istiḥsān* was not significantly different from that of his predecessors except that he often used expressions that were equivalent, yet not identical to *istiḥsān*, such as *aḥabbu ilayya* (more to my liking), instead of *astaḥsinu* (I prefer). The Imam has described *istiḥsān* as a 'special permission' which is to be utilised in order to prevent an evil outcome or to secure the well-being of people.[12] One instance of *istiḥsān* validated by the Imam concerns the case of a laundryman (or dry-cleaner) who is not obliged to pay his customers for materials damaged or stolen from his store. He is like a trustee (*amīn*) who is not under liability (*damān*) to compensate for the loss of such materials. But Imam Mālik held, on the basis of *istiḥsān*, that the laundryman should compensate his customers and this he held to be in the interest of ensuring security and confidence in market transactions.[13]

Imam Mālik also made a leading statement concerning *istiḥsān* when he observed that '*istiḥsān* represents nine-tenths of human knowledge.'[14] Quoting this, Abū Zahrah wrote that in making this observation, Imam Mālik evidently included the broad concept of *maṣlaḥah* under the purview of *istiḥsān*. 'For it is the *maṣlaḥah* which accounts for the larger part of the nine-tenths.'[15] Imam Mālik's remarkable description might seem like an overstatement but if one looks at the essence of *istiḥsān*, which is to find better solutions and alternatives to the ones that are already known, then *istiḥsān* always aims at greater refinement and persistent improvement of the *status quo*. The quest is not only for solutions but for better solutions to the ones that already exist. Imam Mālik's statement is also reminiscent of the relationship of *istiḥsān* with the other proofs of *Sharīʿah*. *Istiḥsān* in its broadest sense, as earlier noted, relates to the entire range of recognised proofs, and seeks to utilise the rich resources of *Sharīʿah* in what should be an incessant search for more refined solutions to issues. Another significant characterisation of *istiḥsān* is that of Asbagh b. Faraj b. Saʿīd al-Mālikī (d. 225/839) who went on record to state that '*istiḥsān* may play a more prominent role than *qiyās* in the advancement of knowledge. For *istiḥsān* is a pillar of knowledge and one who over-indulges in *qiyās* may isolate himself from the *Sunnah*.'[16]

Imam Mālik's characterisation of *istiḥsān* as 'nine-tenths of knowledge' refers not to the individual preference of the jurist which emanates from his personal inclination, but to one which is founded on credible evidence and gives preference to a specific interest (*maṣlaḥah juz'iyyah*) vis-à-vis a general but unsatisfactory *qiyās*. This may be said to be equivalent to giving preference to unrestricted reasoning (*al-istidlāl al-mursal*) over *qiyās*. Ibn Rushd has envisaged that recourse to *istiḥsān* may be more extensive and more frequent than recourse to *qiyās*. This is because *istiḥsān* seeks to discard the extravagance of *qiyās* in the determination of the rules of *Sharīʿah* and validates a departure from it in particular cases—because of evidence that is more effective in those cases.[17]

There are contradictory reports about Imam Aḥmad b. Ḥanbal's (d. 241/ 855) position concerning the validity of *istiḥsān*. One of his disciples is said to have related the following statement from the Imam, which is evidently disparaging of *istiḥsān* and criticises the Ḥanafīs for their advocacy of the doctrine: 'when the followers of Abū Ḥanīfah decide a case in opposition to the ruling of *qiyās* they say 'We prefer this and we abandon *qiyās*,' so they resort to *istiḥsān* in support of whatever they believe.' Then the Imam said 'I follow every ḥadīth that has reached us and do not resort to *qiyās* over and above it.' Qādi Abū Yaʿlā al-Farrā has considered this to be equivalent to a refutation of *istiḥsān* on the part of the Imam. According to yet another observation, what the Imam really meant was to denounce the type of *istiḥsān* not supported by evidence, but that he did not deny the validity of *istiḥsān* that had proper evidential back up.[18]

Ibn Taymiyyah has stated that Aḥmad Ibn Ḥanbal resorted to *istiḥsān* in many places such as in his opinion related by his son, Ṣāliḥ, on limited commenda (*mudārabah*): if the entrepreneur (*mudārib*) disobeys the owner by purchasing what he was not authorised to buy, and he makes a profit, the profit belongs to the owner but the *mudārib* is entitled to a share in it which is proportionate to his labour, unless the profit is exhausted by the labourer's share. The Imam said concerning this: 'I used to hold the opinion that the profit belonged to the owner of the money, then I changed my view and preferred otherwise.' According to another report, Imam Ibn Ḥanbal has held, concerning someone who usurped another person's land and then planted a crop in it, that the crop belonged to the owner of the land who is, however, liable to pay the cultivator for his labour expenses. The ruling here entitles the owner, rather than the cultivator, to the crop, and it draws support from the ḥadīth narrated by Rāfiᶜ b. Khadīj from the Blessed Prophet: 'Whoever plants in other people's land, the crop belongs to the owner of the land but the cultivator is entitled to his labour expenses.'

The normal ruling of qiyās requires that the crop belongs to whoever planted it. Imam Aḥmad b. Ḥanbal's ruling marks a departure from this and it is therefore an instance of *istiḥsān* which is founded in the authority of *Sunnah.*[19]

Al-Āmidī, al-Ṭūfī and also Ibn al-Ḥājib have stated that Imam Ibn Ḥanbal validated *istiḥsān*, while Ibn Qudāmah, a leading Ḥanbalī scholar, has spoken strongly against it. Notwithstanding this, there is evidence to suggest that Imam Ibn Ḥanbal has in fact upheld the validity of *istiḥsān*, for al-Ṭūfī, himself a Ḥanbalī jurist, defined it as a departure from the established law on the basis of valid legal evidence (*dalīl sharᶜī*) and he attributed this principle to Aḥmad Ibn Ḥanbal. It may be noted in passing here that the *istiḥsān* which has been the main target of criticism is the one which the Ḥanafīs have called hidden analogy (*qiyās khafī*). Having said this, the Ḥanbalī *istiḥsān*, like its Mālikī and Ḥanafī counterparts, is signified by a departure from a weaker evidence in favour of a stronger proof. The balance of available evidence suggests that Imam Aḥmad upheld a basically affirmative outlook on *istiḥsān*. This is also the conclusion that Abū Bakr Mīqā has reached, and he has made the observation that the negative reports from the Imam that depict a different picture must therefore be attributed to that variety of *istiḥsān* that is based on unsubstantiated and essentially arbitrary preference. This kind of *istiḥsān* can hardly be said to have been supported by any of the leading Imams, Ibn Ḥanbal included. Mīqā also extended the same assessment to Imam Shāfiᶜī's refutation of *istiḥsān*, and stated that all of the leading Imams, including al-Shāfiʿī, have upheld the basic validity of *istiḥsān*.[20] This view might seem somewhat presumptive, however, given the unequivocal refutation of *istiḥsān* in al-Shāfiʿīs works, *al-Umm* and *al-Risāla*, and his renowned statement that equates *istiḥsān* with caprice and pleasure-seeking (*taladhudh wa hawā*).

NOTES

1. Al-Zarqā, *Al-Madkhal al-Fiqhī al-ʿĀmm*, 6th edition, Damascus, Dār al-Fikr, 1967, I, 88.
2. Abū Sulaymān, *Al-Fikr al-Uṣūlī*, p. 152.
3. Qarāfi, *Tabsirat al-Ḥukkām*. ed. Tāha ʿAbd al-Raūf Saʿd. Cairo: Maktabah Kulliyyāt al-Azhariyyah, 1406/1986, II, 60–61.
4. Al-Bazdawi, *Kashf al-Asrār*, Constantinople, 1307 AH, p. 125.
5. Abū Zahrah, *Abū Ḥanīfah: Ḥayātuh wa ʿAṣruh, Arā'uh wa Fiqhuh*. Cairo: Dār al-Fikr al-ʿArabī, 1366/1947, par. 172; Zarqā, *Al-Madkhal*, I, 87.
6. Bazdawi, *Kashf*, p. 1126.
7. Ibn al-Muqaffaʿ, 'Risālah fi'l-Sahabah,' in Muḥammad Kurd ʿAlī, ed., *Risālah al-Bulaghah*. 4th edn., Cairo, 1954, p. 125.
8. Shaybānī, *Al-Siyar al-Kabīr*. Hyderabad, n.p., 1335 AH, I, 270.
9. Idem, *Al-Aṣl*. Cairo, n.p., 1966–1973, p. 27.
10. Abū Yūsuf, *Kitāb al-Kharāj*. 2nd edn. Cairo, Al-Maṭbaʿah al-Salafiyyah, 1352/1933, pp. 182–183.
11. Ibid., p. 182.
12. Sahnūn, *Al-Mudawwamah al-Kubra*. Cairo, Al-Maktabah al-Khayriyyah, 1324/1909, XVI, 320.
13. Ibid.
14. Shāṭibī, *Muwāfaqāt*, IV, 208.
15. Abū Zahrah, *Uṣūl*, p. 207.
16. Quoted in Shāṭibī, *Muwāfaqāt*, IV, 118.
17. Al-Shāṭibī, *al-Iʿtiṣām*, II, 138; see also al-Husari, *Al-Dawlah wa Siyāsat al-Ḥukm fi'l-Fiqh al-Islāmī*. Vol. 2. Cairo: Maktabah al-Kulliyāt al-Azhariyyah, 1408/1988, p. 83.
18. Al-Farrā, *Al-ʿUddah fī Uṣūl al-Fiqh*. Ed. Aḥmad b. ʿAlī al-Mubarakī, Beirut, Mu'assasah al-Risalah, 1400/1980, II, 489; *Mawsūʿah al-Fiqh al-Islāmī*, Cairo, Dār al-Kitāb al-Miṣrī, 1970, 'Al-Istiḥsān', VI, 43; Abū Sulayman, *Al-Fikr al-Uṣūlī*, p. 285.
19. Ibn Taymiyyah 'Mas'alah al-Istiḥsān', p. 458; an English translation of sections of *Mas'alah al-Istiḥsān* also appears in Ridwan Yūsuf, *The Theory of Istiḥsān*, unpublished Ph.D Dissertation, McGill University, Montreal, 1993, pp. 152ff.
20. Mīqā, *Al-Ra'y*, pp. 403 and 420; Aḥmad Ḥasan, *Analogical Reasoning*, p. 418; *Mawsuʿah* 'Istiḥsān', VI, 43.

CHAPTER THREE

Istiḥsān, Maṣlaḥah and Custom

As a principle of jurisprudence, *istiḥsān* often consists of abandoning *qiyās* in favour of what is deemed to be easier and more accommodating (*arfaq*) to the people. *Istiḥsān*, in other words, is rooted in *maṣlaḥah* and derives its basic argument from it. This common core of identity between *maṣlaḥah* and *istiḥsān* is the focus of Sarakhsī's discussion of *istiḥsān*, which he elaborates by referring to the Qur'ānic text that 'God intends facility and ease for you; He does not intend to put you to hardship.' (Al-Baqarah, 2:185)

يريد الله بكم اليسر ولا يريد بكم العسر

Sarakhsī also quoted three ḥadīths, one of which declared that 'the best of your religion is that which brings ease.'

خير دينكم أيسره

In the second ḥadīth, the Prophet instructed ʿAlī b. Abū Ṭālib and Muʿādh b. Jabal, upon their departure as judges to the Yemen, to 'Make things easier, not difficult, and seek closeness (with the people) not disaffection.'

يسرا ولا تعسرا قربا ولا تنفرا

In the third ḥadīth quoted by al-Sarakhsī, the Prophet highlighted two main features of Islam, one of which is firmness regarding values and principles, and the other is gentleness (*al-rifq*), and instructed the believers to imbue gentleness into Islam and to avoid creating disaffection toward Islam among the servants of God by being harsh and unrelenting:

> Islam is firm [on values], so go into it with gentleness. For the traveller who does not take respite neither gives the camel a break nor cuts the distance short. Do not make the servants of God shun the worship of God.

إن هذا الدين متين فأوغل فيه برفق فإن المنبت لا ظهرا أبقى
ولا أرضا قطع. لا تبغضوا عباد الله عبادة الله

Having discussed the textual evidence in support of *maṣlaḥah* as the anchor of *istiḥsān*, Sarakhsī writes that the essence of *istiḥsān* is 'to abandon hardship in favour of ease and this is a normative principle of Islam (*al-aṣl fī'l-dīn*)'.[1] Whereas Sarakhsī's description of *istiḥsān* has accentuated the substantial parity of *istiḥsān* and *maṣlaḥah*, al-Subkī has highlighted the common ground between *maṣlaḥah* and custom. In al-Subkī's assessment, *maṣlaḥah* is secured through acting upon custom. *Istiḥsān* has thus been characterised as 'departure from the requirement of direct evidence of a general principle in favour of custom in order to secure a *maṣlaḥah*.'[2] From this description, it will be noted that the basic ingredient which is common to *istiḥsān*, *maṣlaḥah* and custom is the removal of hardship (*rafᶜ al-ḥaraj*) and facilitating the affairs of people. According to al-Āmidī, if the underlying custom is generally accepted by the Muslim community (*ummah*) then that would to all intents and purposes be tantamount to their general consensus *ijmāᶜ*. Hence, the evidential basis of *istiḥsān* would no longer be custom but *ijmāᶜ* of the *ummah*.[3] Muṣṭafā al-Zarqā has on the other hand quoted Ibn Rushd and concurred with his assessment that 'for the most part, *istiḥsān* consists of paying attention to the requirements of *maṣlaḥah* and justice.'[4]

In a similar vein, al-Shāṭibī wrote that *istiḥsān* according to the Mālikī school meant giving priority to a particular *maṣlaḥah* vis-à-vis a general principle, and that this in turn involved, as in *maṣlaḥah* itself, reliance on unrestricted reasoning (*al-istidlāl al-mursal*) over *qiyās*. An example of this would be when someone buys goods with an option (*al-khiyār*) reserving for himself the right to ratify or rescind the sale at a later date, and then he dies before he exercises that option. The legal heirs disagree among themselves about whether or not to ratify the proposed purchase. There are two possible solutions, of which one, based on *qiyās*, is to rescind the deal as a matter of principle simply because the buyer's heirs have inherited an option and rejection by some of them is tantamount to rejection by all and thus terminates the option. This might, however, prove detrimental to the seller and an alternative solution is suggested by way of *istiḥsān* which is that acceptance by some is taken as acceptance by all if this means taking the lesser of the two evils, or the less harmful solution. This is the ruling of the Mālikī school, which al-Shāṭibī has upheld. Even if only one of the legal heirs wishes to ratify the purchase and pay the whole of the price, the sale will become binding on the seller. In the event where some of the heirs who wish to ratify the purchase are willing to settle their account with those who disapprove of it—then also the deal should be finalised.[5] The departure in this *istiḥsān* is based on *maṣlaḥah*, which may be to prevent a possible harm and also perhaps to vindicate the integrity of contracts and the basic agreement that has been reached over a sale despite the stipulation of *khiyār*. Another Mālikī jurist, Ibn al-Ḥājib, has disagreed, however, and recorded the view that *istiḥsān* does not proceed in respect of disputed matters. Ibn al-Ḥājib has thus taken a different view of the matter to that of al-Shāṭibī, but my review of the evidence in the following pages suggests that al-Shāṭibī is right in the sense that disputed matters need not be precluded from the purview of *istiḥsān*. The Ḥanafīs have also disagreed with the Mālikī *ijtihād* on this issue, but this is by reference to the established Ḥanafī principle that the option of stipulation (*khiyār al-sharṭ*) is not transferable to heirs. Hence the option expires with the death of the person who initiated it, during the stipulated period, with the result that the contract shall be deemed ratified and the buyer's ownership shall be established over the sold object, if the seller had initiated the option, or the ownership of the heirs of the buyer will be established.[6]

The essence of *maṣlaḥah* pursued by *istiḥsān*, according to al-Shāṭibī, is to remove hardship (*rafᶜ al-ḥaraj*), which is a Qur'ānic principle and one of the cardinal objectives of *Sharīᶜah*. Personal preference and desire have in reality no place in *istiḥsān*. For anyone who indulges in personal preference and does not look into the intent and purpose of the law will have fallen into error and deviated. *Istiḥsān* requires adequate insight into the overall objectives of the law, for it is a means of securing these objectives, especially in cases where applying *qiyās* fails to secure the *maṣlaḥah* or when it leads to prejudice and mischief (*mafsadah*). When this is the case, the *Sharīᶜah* requires that a way be found to prevent this mischief, and this is done by recourse to *istiḥsān*.

But even so, the validity of *qiyās* in principle remains unaffected; it is just that sometimes *qiyās* leads to anomalous situations and fails to secure the intended *maṣlaḥah*. In support of these observations, al-Shāṭibī went on to give examples which included the following:

> A benevolent loan (*qard ḥasan*) is essentially a usurious transaction as it involves exchange of money for money on a deferred basis, but *qard* has been validated nevertheless for the sole purpose of preventing hardship to the people. The same may be said of the sale of *ᶜariyyah*, namely of exchanging wet dates on the tree for dry dates, which partakes of *ribā* (usury), but once again *ᶜariyyah* has been permitted by the *Sunnah* on the grounds of leniency and prevention of hardship. Other examples are commenda partnership (*mudārabah*) and fruit-sharing contract (*musāqāt*) which are anomalous in that the subject matter of the contracts, namely labour and the fruit of the trees respectively, do not exist at the time of contract, yet both have been validated on grounds of leniency and prevention of hardship. Examples given by al-Shāṭibī in the area of devotional matters (*ᶜibādāt*) include the permissibility of *al-jamᶜ*, that is, of performing two *ṣalāhī* (obligatory prayers) such as *maghrib* and *ᶜishā'*, at one and the same time, in difficult situations like traveling and heavy rainfall—and also the permission for the traveller to shorten the *ṣalāh*. Al-Shāṭibī then added that one could refer to numerous examples of concessions (*al-tarakhkhusāt*) in *Sharīᶜah*, all of which are predicated on the attainment of benefit and the prevention of prejudice and hardship. To follow the normal rules of *Sharīᶜah* in such situations leads to hardship, and *istiḥsān* serves as a means of preventing this.[7]

Although *istiḥsān* closely identifies with *maṣlaḥah*, the two are not identical in the sense that *istiḥsān* is tied up either to *qiyās* or to the other proofs of *Sharīᶜah*. *Istiḥsān* in other words does not operate independently from the other proofs of *Sharīᶜah*. But this is not necessarily the case with *maṣlaḥah*, which can often consist of an original formula without it having to be tied to a precedent or to another proof. Whereas *maṣlaḥah* is normative, stands on its own feet, and can bring independent legislation, *istiḥsān* tends to operate within the given terms of existing law and seeks only to improve it from within. *Maṣlaḥah*, in other words, is not tied to *qiyās* and does not involve the technicality of working its way through the materials of the existing legal *status quo*. *Istiḥsān* is basically invoked in exceptional situations and anomalies that are encountered in the implementation of existing law. It might be used as a formula to provide an alternative solution but one that is not totally founded on personal opinion without basis in the recognised proofs of *Sharīᶜah*.[8]

NOTES

1. Al-Sarakhsī, *Mabsūṭ*, X, 145.
2. Al-Subkī, *Jamʿ al-Jawāmiʿ fī'l-Uṣūl*. 2nd edn, Cairo, Muṣṭafā al-Bābī al-Ḥalabī, 1365 AH, II, 360. See also al-Shāṭibī, *Muwāfaqāt*, IV, 206.
3. Al-Āmidī, *Al-Iḥkām fī Uṣūl al-Aḥkām*. Ed. ʿAbd al-Razzāq ʿAfīfī, Beirut, Al-Maktab al-Islāmī, 1402/1982, IV, 156; Mīqā, *Al-Ra'y*, p. 400; *Mawsu'ah*, 'Istiḥsān', VI, 38.
4. Al-Zarqā, *Al-Madkhal*, I, 88.
5. Al-Shāṭibī, *Muwāfaqāt*, IV, 206; Abū Zahrah, 'Taʿliq ʿala Mawduʿ al-Istiḥsān wa'l-Masālih al-Mursalah,' in *Al-Majlis al-Aʿla li-Riʿāyat al-Funun, Usbuʿ al-Fiqh al-Islāmī*, Damascus, n.p., 1380, p. 362; al-Mashāt, *Al-Jawāhir al-Thamīnah*. Ed. ʿAbd al-Wahhāb Ibrāhīm Abū Sulaymān, Beirut, Dār al-Gharb al-Islāmī, 1406/1986, p. 221.
6. *The Mejelle: Being An English Translation of Majallah al-Ahkam el-Adliya* by C.R. Tyser. Lahore, Law Publishing Company, 1967, (Art. 306); Zarqā, *Al-Madkhal*, I, 105.
7. Al-Shāṭibī, *Muwāfaqāt*, IV, 206–207.
8. Cf. Al-Zuḥaylī, *Uṣūl al-Fiqh al-Islāmī*. Damascus, Dār al-Fikr li'l Ṭibāʿah wa'l-Tawziʿ wa'l-Nashr, 1406/1986, p. 740; Shaʿbān, *Uṣūl al-Fiqh al-Islāmī*. Kuwait, Jāmiʿah al-Kuwait, n.d., p. 156.

CHAPTER FOUR

Types of *Istiḥsān*

As already indicated, *istiḥsān* is divided into two main types: analogical (*istiḥsān al-qiyāsī*), and exceptional (*istiḥsān al-istithnā'ī*). Whereas the former is a monolithic category, the latter is sub-divided into a number of other types depending on the nature of its underlying evidence. Both types involve abandoning an existing rule for an alternative rule, but in the case of analogical *istiḥsān* the move is from one *qiyās* to another *qiyās*, whereas in the case of exceptional *istiḥsān*, an exception is made to an existing rule (*ḥukm*), whether of *qiyās* or another proof, in favour of a preferable solution. In both types, the departure is warranted because the application of an existing rule to a particular case leads to a result which is at odds with the requirements of a clear text (*naṣṣ*), consensus (*ijmā*ᶜ), necessity (*ḍarūrah*) and custom (ᶜ*urf*).

A ruling of *qiyās* may be abandoned, as Sarakhsī explained, because *qiyās* is not devoid of error and misunderstanding, and it is with the aid of guidance from the text and *ijmā*ᶜ that the error is identified and then corrected through *istiḥsān*.[1] This can be seen in the following pages where various types of *istiḥsān* are discussed and illustrated. The examples chosen below are mainly concerned with civil transactions (*mu*ᶜ*āmalāt*) and serve to show more clearly the role that *istiḥsān* has played in the development of *fiqh*.

A. Analogy-Based *Istiḥsān (al-Istiḥsān al-Qiyāsī)*

This type of *istiḥsān* involves a departure in a particular case from an obvious analogy (*qiyās jalī*) that would apply to similar cases in favour of an alternative analogy (*qiyās khafī*) because of stronger evidence that demands such a departure. The alternative ruling here is more subtle and less obvious than the first.

(1) Under Ḥanafī law, the *waqf* (charitable endowment) of cultivated land includes the transfer of all the ancillary rights attached to the property, such as the right of water (*ḥaqq al-shurb*), right of passage (*ḥaqq al-murūr*) and the right of flow (*ḥaqq al-masīl*) even if these are not explicitly mentioned in the instrument of *waqf*. This ruling is based on *qiyās khafī* (or *istiḥsān*) as I shall presently explain. It is a rule of the Islamic law of contract, including the contract of sale, that the object of contract must be clearly identified in detail. What is not specified in the contract, in other words, is not included therein. Now if one draws a direct analogy (i.e. *qiyās jalī*) between sale and *waqf*—as both involve transfer of ownership—one must conclude that the attached rights can only be included in the *waqf* if they are explicitly identified. It is, however, argued that such an analogy will lead to inequitable results: the *waqf* of cultivated land, without its ancillary rights, would frustrate the basic purpose of *waqf*, which is to facilitate the use of the property for charitable purposes. To avoid hardship, recourse to an alternative analogy, that is to *qiyās khafī*, is therefore warranted. The hidden analogy in this case is to draw a parallel not with the contract of sale, but with the contract of lease (*ijārah*). For both of these involve transfer of usufruct (*intifāᶜ*). Since usufruct is the essential purpose of *ijārah*, this contract is valid, on the authority of a ḥadīth, even without a clear reference to the usufruct. This alternative analogy with *ijārah* enables one to say that *waqf* that is validly concluded subsumes the attached rights to the property even if these have not been specified in the instrument of *waqf*.[2]

(2) To give another example, supposing person A buys a house in a single transaction from persons B and C at a price of 40,000 rials payable on instalments. A pays the first instalment of 2,000 rials to B assuming that B will hand over C's portion to him. But before this happens, B loses the 2,000 and the question arises as to who should suffer the loss. By applying *qiyās jalī*, B and C should share the loss. For this is a case of joint debt (*al-dayn al-mushtarak*) which means that B received the money on behalf of the partnership and not for himself alone. Their position in sharing the loss, in other words, is analogous to their status as partners in the first place. But by applying *istiḥsān*, only B, who received the money, suffers the loss and it is deductable from his portion of the whole price of 40,000. For C, although a partner, was basically under no obligation to obtain his portion of the

2,000 from B. It was only his right/privilege and he was at liberty to waive it. C's portion of the 2,000 rials would consequently become a part of the remainder of the price (or the debt) that A owes to both. Only B is therefore to suffer the loss. This solution is based on a subtle analogy with the rule that one who is under no obligation should not have to pay any compensation either.[3]

(3) It is a recognised principle of law that a person is only answerable for his confession to the extent of his own right, not that of another person. Thus if a person confesses that he and his brother are indebted to someone else, he binds only himself but not his brother, if his brother denies it. Similarly, if a person claims that he is the representative (*wakīl*) of a creditor, who is absent, for recovering his loan, and the debtor confirms this, the debtor may be asked to pay the debt to the *wakīl*, on the basis of his own acknowledgment. This also applies to the case of someone who deposits something to the safekeeping of another and then disappears. Another person later claims that he is the *wakīl* of the absentee to collect his deposit, and the depositary confirms this. Obvious analogy (*qiyās jalī*) to the case of the recovery of debt here requires that the depositary should be bound to deliver the deposit to the *wakīl*.

If one applies *istiḥsān*, however, the depositary will not be required to hand over the deposit to the *wakīl* even though the former acknowledges the latter's representation. This is because it is possible that the depositor will later appear and deny the alleged agency at a time when his deposit might have disappeared and perished, especially when his right is attached to the deposit in rem. This is unlike a debt in which the creditor's right is a charge on the person (*dhimmah*) of the debtor, which is amenable to substitution. If the creditor appears and denies the agency, the debtor is liable to pay him, because the alleged agency is not established and the creditor's right remains intact. The debtor will have, in effect, paid the alleged agent out of his own property, because his acknowledgement of that agency is valid in respect of his own assets only.

As for the deposit (*al-waḍīʿah*), the owner's right is attached to the actual object, not to the person (*dhimmah*) of the depositary. Hence the latter's acknowledgement of the alleged agency is an admission on his part to hand over the property of another person to a third party. Thus it is an admission against another person, not against himself. If it is enforced, it would amount to the renunciation of the right of the owner by the mere acknowledgement of a person other than himself.[4]

(4) In a mortgage transaction, the creditor-mortgagee is liable to

compensate for the loss of the mortgaged property in his possession. But in the case where the creditor-mortgagee has absolved the debtor-mortgagor of the obligation of repaying the loan, he is not held liable to compensate for the loss of the mortgaged property. The reason for this is that a trustee is not liable for the loss of the property in his custody unless he is at fault or negligent. Supposing that the above-mentioned creditor had not waived his claim to the sum lent to the mortgagor, all he would have had to bear would be to absolve the mortgagor from the obligation of repayment. Should one then punish him for his act of generosity, absolving the mortgagor of the obligation to repay the loan? Or would it be preferable to treat this case as analogous to that of a trustee? Here is a subtle analogy that is resorted to in order to avoid the grave injustice that would result from the application of obvious analogy. The obvious analogy (*al-qiyās al-ẓāhir*) in this case requires that the mortgagee should be liable to the mortgagor to compensate the latter for the loss of the mortgaged property, as the act of absolvence (*al-ibrā'*) is considered here to be analogous to the recovery of debt (*al-istīfā'*): In *istīfā'* the mortgaged property remains guaranteed until it is returned to the mortgagor.[5]

(5) The distinction between the two types of *qiyās*, namely obvious analogy and hidden analogy, may not be self-evident and differentiating one from the other may well be a matter of individual *ijtihād*—as the following example will show:

> The guardian of property (*walī ʿala'l-māl*) is authorised to conclude certain transactions on behalf of his ward but he does not have the same authority with regard to certain other transactions. The Ḥanafīs accept that the guardian is authorised to transfer the property of his ward by way of deposit (*al-idāʿ*), which is basically for safekeeping, but it is not valid for him to repay the debt he might owe himself from the property of his ward. The question then arises as to whether the guardian is entitled to mortgage the property of his ward. As a form of transaction, a mortgage is a hybrid between deposit (*al-waḍīʿah*) and debt repayment (*īfā' al-dayn*): it has a facet in common with deposit as both mortgage and deposit involve transfer of possession to a third party, and it has an aspect in common with debt repayment as in the event of the debtor/mortgagor's inability to repay his debt, the mortgagee is entitled to sell the property to recover his loan. There are thus two conflicting analogies involved in the attempt to derive a ruling that would determine the guardian's authority with regard to mortgaging the property of his ward. One by drawing an analogy with deposit, which would validate the mortgage, and the other by drawing an analogy with debt repayment, with the result that the mortgage in question is *ultra vires*. Imam Abū Ḥanīfah and his disciple al-Shaybānī have held the first to be a *qiyās khafī* and the second to be *qiyās jalī*,

but the other two disciples of the Imam, namely Abū Yūsuf and Zufar, have held the analogy with debt repayment to be *qiyās jalī* and the one with deposit to be in the nature of *qiyās khafī*. Zakī al-Dīn Shaʿbān has considered the second of these two positions to be more accurate and explained that the analogy between mortgage and deposit is *qiyās jalī*. For this is what is likely to occur to the *mujtahid* in the first place but he might later be inclined to think of drawing a parallel between mortgage and debt repayment, in which case he will have attempted *qiyās khafī* or *istiḥsān*. The initial analogy is said to be the one which is contrary to *istiḥsān*.[6] This example serves to show that the distinction between the two analogies that are involved in *istiḥsān*, namely the obvious and the hidden, is not always a matter of certainty and this may, in the more complex cases at least, cast doubt on the very substance of analogical *istiḥsān*. The question naturally arises as to whether in such situations one might be dealing with just one methodology, namely that of *qiyās*, and nothing else.

B. Textually-Based *Istiḥsān (al-Istiḥsān bi'l-Naṣṣ)*

This type of *istiḥsān* consists of abandoning a principle or rule that would normally be applicable to the issue at hand for an alternative ruling for which support can be found in the text of the Qur'ān or ḥadīth. An example of this is the forward sale of *salam* which is anomalous as it fails to satisfy one of the requirements of a valid sale, namely that its subject matter must be physically present at the time of contract. But *salam* has been validated by the express terms of ḥadīth, notwithstanding the non-existence of its subject matter at the time of contract. The general rules of contract (or *qiyās*), in other words, invalidate *salam* but the *Sunnah* approves it, as the following ḥadīth provides:

> Whoever concludes *salam*, let him do so over a specified measure, specified weight and specified period of time.[7]

من أسلف فليسلف في كيل معلوم
ووزن معلوم إلى أجل معلوم

The general rule that the subject matter of sale must exist at the time of contract is also based on the authority of a ḥadīth. In this ḥadīth the Prophet instructed a Companion, Ḥakīm b. Ḥizām, who asked whether he could sell a commodity prior to purchasing it himself, and the Prophet told him to 'sell not what is not with you.'[8]

لا تبع ما ليس عندك

This requirement is evidently not satisfied in *salam*.

There are thus two rulings in the ḥadīth, one of which represents the normal principle of the contract of sale, and the other which is concerned with a particular type of sale; the former would proscribe *salam* whereas the latter validates it. It is then said that *salam* has been validated by way of *istiḥsān* which is contrary to *qiyās*. This is known as *Istiḥsān al-Sunnah* and it signifies abandoning a legal ruling based on *qiyās* in favour of another ruling that is contrary thereto, and the new ruling is authorised by the *Sunnah*.[9]

For another illustration of the textually-based *istiḥsān*, one may refer to the subject of bequest. The Qur'ān validated making a bequest in favour of one's parents and relatives (II:180) despite it being anomalous to the normal rules of *Sharīʿah*. This is because a bequest consists of transfer of ownership after the death of the testator. It is not permissible, in other words, to postpone transfer of ownership to a time when the person who transfers it is no longer the owner. Since a bequest, although made while the testator was alive, becomes effective only after his death, it is said to be basically *ultra vires* and tantamount to interference in the rights of the legal heirs. But the Qur'ān has validated making a bequest nevertheless, and the *Sunnah* has also confirmed this but stipulated that a bequest is valid up to a maximum of one third of one's estate. In this example, too, there are two opposing rules, one of general application and the other which is specific to bequests. The Ḥanafīs have then stated that the Qur'ān has permitted bequests by way of *istiḥsān*, that is contrary to *qiyās*. It sets aside, in other words, the general principle in favour of an exception which aims for the fair distribution of wealth in a family, especially when the specific rules of inheritance may lead to a situation where a relative is barred from inheritance on technical grounds, so to speak, but is otherwise in need of assistance.[10]

The option of stipulation (*khiyār al-sharṭ*) also represents an instance of textually-based *istiḥsān*. *Khiyār al-sharṭ* is basically *ultra vires* and disagreeable to the normal principles of contract. As a general rule, a contract becomes binding as of the moment it is validly concluded. *Khiyār al-sharṭ* on the other hand entitles the contracting parties to postpone that moment and suspend the legal consequences of contract by means of stipulation to a later date. But since *khiyār al-sharṭ* has been clearly validated in the ḥadīth, on grounds of equity and fairness—which is to provide one or both of the contracting parties with an opportunity to decide whether or not to ratify the contract—it is then said that the *Sunnah* validates *khiyār al-sharṭ* by way of *istiḥsān*, which consists of making an exception to the general rule of the immediacy of contracts.[11]

C. *Istiḥsān* and *Ijmāᶜ*

An exception to the general rule of law may be based on the authority of *ijmāᶜ*, in which case it is said that the *istiḥsān* in question is validated by *ijmāᶜ*. To illustrate this one may refer to *istiṣnāᶜ* or the manufacturing contract which is contrary to the normal rules of contract. When someone places an order for some goods to be made, a contract is concluded in the absence of its subject matter and nothing changes hands at the time. Yet the anomaly of *istiṣnāᶜ* has been ignored and it has been validated by general consensus, which is why it is said that *istiṣnāᶜ* is contrary to systematic reasoning or *qiyās*.[12] This is known as *istiḥsān al-ijmāᶜ* and it signifies departure from what *qiyās* requires to an alternative ruling is established by general consensus, or *ijmāᶜ*.[13]

For a second illustration, one may refer to the example al-Shāṭibī has given of cases in which the partial destruction of something may render a person liable for compensation of the whole. It is thus stated that one who mutilates the tail of the horse that a judge rode for official duty is liable to pay the full price of the horse in compensation. This is because it will be below the dignity of judicial office for the judge to ride the same horse again. Liability for full compensation, as opposed to a partial compensation which is commensurate to the loss here, is contrary to the normal rule that would render the person liable only for partial compensation. The departure here is in the nature of *istiḥsān* which is validated by *ijmāᶜ*.[14]

On a similar note, there is consensus among the *ᶜulamā'* that one who destroys one item of a pair such as a shoe, or one of the two panels of a door, or damages a part of something so that it is considered defective as a whole, will be liable to pay compensation for both pairs or the whole of a matching set as the case may be. The ruling of consensus here represents a departure from the rules of *qiyās* which would require compensation only for the part that is actually damaged or destroyed.[15]

Istiḥsān that is founded in *ijmāᶜ* closely resembles that which is authorized by custom, so much so that some writers are inclined to subsume custom-based *istiḥsān* under the general umbrella of *ijmāᶜ*.

For it is said that the difference between the two fades into insignificance and the issue falls under the stronger of the two proofs, namely that of *ijmā*ᶜ. Ibn ᶜĀbidīn has thus commented: in the event where a rule of custom is in partial conflict with a general ruling (ᶜ*āmm*) of the text, the latter may be specified by custom only when the custom in question is general. For it is only the general (ᶜ*urf*) that can operate as a specifier of the text and takes priority over *qiyās*—such as in the case of manufacturing order (*istiṣnā*ᶜ), and also of entry into the public bath.[16] It thus appears that Ibn ᶜĀbidīn has effectively subsumed custom-based *istiḥsān* under *istiḥsān* that is validated by general consensus.

D. *Istiḥsān* and Necessity *(Darūrah)*

One finds many examples, in the works of Ḥanafī jurists in particular, where a person may be exceptionally permitted to deal with the property of another person without the permission or authorisation of the latter. The subject here falls under the *fiqh* topic of *al-fuḍūlī* (bona fide but unauthorised agent). The normal rules would disallow such a person from interfering with the property of others, but the activities of a *fuḍūlī* are often validated on grounds of *istiḥsān* founded on necessity and prevention of harm. Note also the following examples:

(1) It is lawful for either a father or a son, whichever the case may be, to sell the property of the other if he is afflicted with illness, to the extent of what is necessary for medication and treatment, even without the latter's permission. The normal rule does not allow interference in the property of another person without his permission, but a departure from this rule is here validated on grounds of necessity and *istiḥsān*.

(2) The deposit holder (*al-wadī*ᶜ) is normally not entitled to spend out of the property that is entrusted to him without the permission of the depositor or a judge. But he may do so if the depositor is out of reach and it is also difficult to obtain a judicial order for the purpose.

(3) A traveling companion may spend what is necessary out of the property of his co-traveller who has fallen ill or died without his permission or the permission of his legal heirs.[17] It is reported that when a student of Muḥammad b. Ḥasan al-Shaybānī died, al-Shaybānī sold his books in order to meet the burial expenditures. Someone told al-Shaybānī that his student had not left a will to authorise the sale, to which he recited the Qur'ānic *āyah* that 'God

knows the miscreant from the well-wisher'—(Al-Baqarah, 2:220) and he was right. Ibn Qayyim al-Jawziyyah wrote that only a most parochial jurist would advise against what al-Shaybānī had done on the specious analysis that it was unauthorised interference in someone else's property. The truth remains, however, that doing nothing in that situation would have meant inactivity in the face of prejudice.[18]

(4) In the event of the absence of his adult and affluent son, the father who is in need of support may sell only the movable property of his son for his own needs, that is by way of *istiḥsān* according to Imam Abū Ḥanīfah. The two disciples of Abū Ḥanīfah, al-Shaybānī and Abū Yūsuf have, however, disagreed and maintained the view that the father's authority of guardianship (*wilāyah*) over the son terminates with the latter's attainment of majority and prudence. But even Imam Abū Ḥanīfah, who upheld the opposite by way of *istiḥsān*, disallowed the father to sell the immovable property of his absent son.[19]

(5) The legally competent heirs of the deceased may spend, by way of *istiḥsān*, on their minor relatives who have no legal executor (*wasī*) what is necessary out of their own (children's) property without any authorisation. By the same token, when a mosque is without a caretaker but is the recipient of income from a charitable endowment (*waqf*), the people of the locality may spend out of this income to repair any damage in the mosque or to build a fence around it.[20]

(6) According to an established rule of *fiqh*, the testimony of non-Muslims against Muslims is not admissible as this is held to be the implied meaning of the Qur'ānic text 'and God does not grant to disbelievers authority over the believers' (al-Nisā', 4:141). However, in the following two situations exceptions to the normal rules are made on grounds of necessity: when a non-Muslim claims to be the sole heir and son of his deceased father, also a non-Muslim, and he then attempts to collect a debt that a Muslim had owed to his father. However, when the Muslim debtor denies that the claimant was the son of the deceased, the claimant brings two non-Muslim witnesses to prove his status and claim. To apply the normal rule, or analogy as it is said, would disqualify the non-Muslim witnesses giving testimony against a Muslim, but necessity and *istiḥsān* would admit their testimony. This is because paternity is established through marriage and birth and Muslims usually do not attend these occasions when they occur among non-Muslims. Hence it becomes necessary, in order to serve justice, that non-Muslim witnesses are admitted in this case.

The second situation where a similar exception is granted may be illustrated as follows. A Muslim claims to have been appointed executor (*waṣī*) by a non-Muslim; then he presents a Muslim who owed his deceased principal a debt. The debtor admits the debt but denies both the death of the principal party and the appointment of the executor. Now if two non-Muslim witnesses testify and affirm the death and executorship, their testimony will be admissible even if it is against a Muslim. This ruling of *istiḥsān* is founded on the analysis that the death of non-Muslims and the appointment of an executor by them is usually seen by their own people, not by Muslims, and if the non-Muslim's testimony is denied in this case, it may amount to a miscarriage of justice, which must be avoided.

Whereas the Ḥanafīs have exceptionally validated the testimony of non-Muslims against Muslims in the above cases, Ibn Taymiyyah has generally held the view that their testimony is admissible in all cases of necessity and whenever this would serve the cause of justice and the protection of the people's rights. A follower of revealed religion, one of the *Ahl al-Kitāb*, may be trustworthy and enjoy good reputation, which a Muslim may not. Since the criterion for the admissibility of witnesses is their honesty and trustworthiness, not necessarily religious following, the testimony of non-Muslims must be admitted whenever they inspire trust and confidence and in all cases of necessity. While stating this, Ibn Taymiyya and his disciple, Ibn Qayyim, have referred to the fact that the Prophet employed a non-Muslim guide when he migrated to Medina and he trusted him and paid him for his service despite the dangerous journey that lay ahead. Hence it appears that the judge and ruler must not turn away from truth when it becomes known to them from any source and by anyone.[21]

(7) A similar example of *istiḥsān* based on necessity is the case of a two-storey building owned jointly by two different people. The building is dilapidated or destroyed. Against the basic tendency in Islamic law to defend the total independence of each proprietor, the owner of the upper storey can force the owner of the lower storey to rebuild so that he may do the same. This is the ruling of *istiḥsān* which draws an exception to the normal rule recognising the total independence of the owner.

In the *fatwas* of the latter-day jurists one finds similar restrictions imposed on the free use of private property due to damage caused to neighbours. Thus a bakery owner is restricted on account of the smoke he creates, and this is described as an instance of *istiḥsān* based on necessity against the former authoritative ruling (*ẓāhir al-riwāya*) of the Ḥanafī school.[22]

E. *Istiḥsān* based on *Maṣlaḥah*

This variety of *istiḥsān* applies to any issue that can be determined under a general text or an established ruling, but then considerations of *maṣlaḥah* warrant an exception to the general rule, as may be illustrated below:

(1) According to the established rules of fiqh, the contract of crop-sharing (muzāraʿah) terminates with the death of both or one of the contracting parties. This rule has, however, been set aside in the event where the owner of an agricultural property dies at a time when the crop is still growing. The contract is thus allowed to remain valid until the harvest is taken, for otherwise the farmer is likely to suffer losses and there may be no one to care for the crops.

(2) The Shāfiʿī jurist and Mufti of Palestine, Khayr al-Dīn al Ramlī (1585-1671) has recorded instances of *istiṣlāḥ* which resemble *istiḥsān* in his renowned *Fatāwā al-Khayriyya*. An example of this, recorded by Ramlī, relates to dilapidated *waqf* properties that no one is willing to exchange for other properties. Al-Ramlī says that the latter-day jurists went so far as to permit an exchange of the *waqf* for cash 'on the ground of *istiṣlāḥ*, or concern for the public good', and Ramlī himself enthusiastically approved of it. This is a typical example, one might add, of a *maṣlaḥah*-based *istiḥsān*, which the Shāfiʿī jurist has, however, subsumed under *istiṣlāḥ*. The difference between *istiḥsān* and *istiṣlāḥ,* in so far as it relates to our example, is the framework of the proposed ruling. If the departure marks an exception from an existing law while the law itself remains valid, it is a case of *istiḥsān*. *Istiṣlāḥ*, on the other hand, is a more appropriate vehicle for original legislation that is not tied to another ruling. It is probably due to the different scholastic perspective of the Shāfiʿī school that the present example is subsumed under *istiṣlāḥ*.

(3) The established rules of *fiqh* concerning liability for loss (*al-ḍamān*) hold the trustee (*amīn*) liable for possible destruction or loss of the property in his custody when he is negligent but not otherwise. This would absolve a craftsman or a tailor, known as a shared employee (*al-ajīr al-mushtarak*), for example, of liability if the material that was entrusted to him by the client is stolen or destroyed without any negligence in his part. The disciples of Abū-Ḥanīfah, Abū

Yūsuf and al-Shaybānī and also Imam Mālik, as noted earlier, have, however, held the trustee responsible for the loss or destruction of what is placed in his custody unless it can be shown that it was totally beyond his control, such as in the case of fire and earthquake. The ruling here represents a departure from the normal rule that the trustee, like the depositary (*waḍīᶜ*), is not liable to compensation unless he violates or neglects the terms of the trust and fails to exercise due care. This departure is justified on grounds of public interest so that trustees and tradesman exercise greater care in safeguarding people's property.[23] The Mālikīs have widened this application of the *maṣlaḥah* vis-à-vis *qiyās* in holding liable for compensation not only tradesmen who fall under the definition of trustee but also those who may not fit that description. The ship owner, the owner of the public bath, trade agents and brokers (*al-samāsirah al-mushtarakīn*) and the transporter of foodstuff (*ḥammāl al-ṭaᶜām*) are all liable to compensate for loss of the property of their clients in order to ensure greater care and also public confidence in market activities.

The proponents of *istiḥsān* have differentiated between the private employee (*al-ajīr al-khāṣṣ*) who sells his entire time to his employer and does not divide it with work for anyone else, such as a servant or a driver and the like, and the common employee (*al-ajīr al-mushtarak* or *al-ajīr-al-ᶜāmm*), who sells his labour in a line of business to anyone who asks for it such as a dyer, a baker, or a carpenter etc. The proponents of *istiḥsān* maintain that the common employee is liable for the people's properties that are placed in his custody, if they perish or damage, except in cases of uncontrollable calamities, such as fire or earthquake. This is to ensure that the common employee does not accept work that is in excess of his capacity, out of the urge to make more money, thus exposing the properties placed in his custody to destruction and loss by keeping them for a longer period. Whereas the Mālikīs have adopted this ruling on the ground of *maṣlaḥah,* the Ḥanafīs have done the same on the ground of *maṣlaḥah*-based *istiḥsān.*[24]

(4) Another illustration of the *maṣlaḥah*-based *istiḥsān* which represents an exception to the general principles is the ruling which permits an idiot (*safīh*) who is under interdiction to make a bequest or establish a charitable endowment (*waqf*) regardless of the interdiction. The normal rules of *fiqh* do not permit such a person to make charitable dispensations but the exception here is based on the rationale that both bequest and *waqf* involve the transfer of assets after the death of the testator/and *waqīf* and they are in the nature of preserv-

ing, rather than the wasteful expenditure of, the existent assets—hence they are validated by way of *istiḥsān,* which encourages charity and good work.[25]

(5) Another example is when someone sees a goat that is without its owner and has suffered an injury that is likely to cause its death, and with a view to prevent its loss, the observer slaughters it at his own initiative without the owner's permission. The normal rules would make him liable for compensating the owner, but not liable under the rules of *istiḥsān* based on *maṣlaḥah.*[26]

(6) It is of interest to note one of the instances of modern legislation which originated in what may be seen as a *maṣlaḥah*-based *istiḥsān.* I refer here to the Egyptian law (No. 344) of 1956 which regulated the construction and demolition of urban properties. The government was empowered under this law to supervise the construction and demolition of private buildings which were often motivated by commercial considerations in disregard to their effect on national wealth, urban planning and the environment. Old buildings of historical value were often demolished by their owners to be replaced by commercially more profitable structures, and so were relatively new buildings that were destroyed and replaced by more recent designs. The government was thus granted powers under this law to regulate the situation in line with considerations of public interest and obstruct, if necessary, unwarranted demolition activities of private buildings through the issue of licenses for the purpose. The explanatory memorandum that was attached to that law quoted in support the juristic *fatwā,* based on *istiḥsān,* to the effect that the owner of a house in a prosperous district may be stopped from demolishing his property in due consideration to the interest and welfare of local residents. The ruling here signifies a departure from the normal principle which grants the owner unrestricted freedom as to the manner in which he deals with his own property.[27]

F. *Istiḥsān* Based on Custom

This type of *istiḥsān* applies to customary matters, including transactions and contracts, and rules that have found general acceptance even if they represent a departure from the normal principles and established positions of *Sharīʿah.* Many examples of this can be found in the works of Ḥanafī *fiqh,* especially including the following:

(1) With regard to contractual stipulations, the Ḥanafīs maintain that conditions and stipulations inserted into a contract that are in

disharmony with the essence of the contract are voidable (*fāsid*) and vitiate the contract, especially in the case of contracts involving exchange of values (*ᶜuqūd muᶜāwadāt al-māliyyah*). But the Ḥanafīs have departed from this position in the event where the stipulation in question is accepted by general custom. A stipulation of this kind will consequently be upheld by way of *istiḥsān* that represents a departure from the normal rule, on the strength of its acceptance by customary practice. Note, for example, the established rule of *fiqh* which designates *waqf* as a permanent endowment that can only be instituted for immovable property. Movable property, which is liable to destruction and loss, is consequently not to be assigned in *waqf*. This general rule has, however, been set aside by the Ḥanafī jurist al-Shaybānī, who validated the *waqf* of movable goods such as books, tools and weapons simply because popular custom accepted this. The customary concession here encourages charity and good work without undue restrictions on grounds of the attributes of the property involved.[28] Given the somewhat restrictive regime of *waqf* under the rules of *fiqh*, further relaxation of the normal rules pertaining to *waqf* is commendable. I shall take up this issue again but suffice it to note here that in view of the changes that have taken place under statutory legislation in many present day Muslim countries, especially the fact that land reform laws in recent times have led to the splitting up of large family estates into smaller units, *waqf* of smaller units of landed property has often proved to be uneconomical. A change of direction may therefore be advisable in order to inject fresh impetus into the institution and legal regime of *waqf* under present circumstances.[29]

(2) Entry to the public bath and the fixed fee charged for it is another example of *istiḥsān* validated by popular custom. Strict conformity to the established rules of sale requires that the subject matter of sale is accurately defined and quantified. However, popular custom has departed from this rule and the user of the public bath is charged a fixed fee without any agreement on the amount of water that is used or the duration of stay. General custom has disapproved of quantifying the amount of water in advance, which is seen as somewhat demeaning and in disharmony with the spirit of generosity and latitude that the *Sunnah* of the Prophet has generally recommended.[30]

(3) The Ḥanafīs have also ruled that the right of water (*ḥaqq al-shurb*) may not be sold on its own, that is, independently of the agricultural land irrigated by it, because of ignorance of the quantity involved and also uncertainty about the ownership of water not in one's possession nor custody. But some Ḥanafī jurists have held it to

be permissible by way of *istiḥsān* founded on customary approval of this sale. The normal rules of sale thus proscribe the sale in question, but it is exceptionally validated on the basis of *istiḥsān* and *ᶜurf*.[31] In the modern day context, one may overlook this *istiḥsān* and return to the normal rules, which is now possible due to the availability of measuring tools such as water meters. Water that is consumed in public baths, or for other similar purposes, can now be measured, and there should, in principle, be no objection to the sale of water by volume, especially in places where the necessary facilities are easily available. This shows once again that the rules of custom can be liable to change due to new developments in industry and commerce, and changes of lifestyle in congested urban areas.

As a matter of fact custom-based *istiḥsān* finds extensive application in commercial contracts and transactions. This is perhaps most evident in regard to contracts that involve a certain amount of risk-taking and *gharar* (partial ignorance over the precise specification of counter-values) and even *ribā*. If the rules of *gharar* and *ribā* are strictly enforced, the smooth flow of market transactions is likely to be affected, and it is often in such cases that customary practice intervenes and validates transactions wherein a certain degree of *gharar* or *ribā* is tolerated, contrary to normal rules. This is also the case with regard to the determination of the time and place of delivery in contracts of sale, which must be precisely determined according to normal rules, but a certain amount of ambiguity is often tolerated on grounds of *istiḥsān*. Imam Mālik has validated many varieties of time-bound sales (*buyuᶜ al-ājāl*) on this basis, so much so that he has been criticised for it. Yet it is fairly obvious that this variety of *istiḥsān* is premised on the Qur'ānic principle of the removal of hardship (*rafᶜ al-ḥaraj*), which is valid *Sharīᶜah* evidence, and not, as it were, an arbitrary and unwarranted indulgence in *ra'y*.[32]

(4) Suppose that A swears that he will not enter into a house (*al-bayt*) where B enters. But then A and B enter into a mosque together. The question whether A has violated his oath has been answered in the negative, which is to say that A is not held to be a violator of his oath. The explanation provided is this: notwithstanding the fact that the Qur'ān uses the word '*bayt*' in reference to the mosque (cf. al-Nūr, 24:36), Arabic speaking people customarily do not use this word in reference to the mosque (*masjid*). Based on this customary usage, and by recourse to *istiḥsān* that is founded on it, A has not violated his oath by entering the mosque with B. The Mālikīs and Ḥanafīs have approved of this conclusion.[33]

As stated earlier, some *ᶜulamā'* have recorded the view that *istiḥsān* based on general custom is to all intents and purposes equivalent to *istiḥsān* based on *ijmāᶜ*. Thus according to al-Āmidi, if the custom in question is one on which there is general agreement among the people and community leaders (*ahl al-hall wa'l-ᶜaqd*), then this is equivalent to *ijmāᶜ*. In the event where the custom is not generally recognised, then abandoning *sharᶜī* evidence because of it will not be valid.[34]

G. *Istiḥsān* and the Removal of Hardship *(rafᶜ al-ḥaraj)*

Istiḥsān premised on considerations of equity (*iḥsān*) and the removal of hardship may be illustrated in the following examples:

(1) One may refer to a case of inheritance known as *al-Mushtarakah* (the apportioned) which took place early in the time of the Caliph ᶜUmar ibn al-Khaṭṭāb. A woman died leaving behind two uterine and two germane brothers, her mother and her husband. The strict rules of inheritance would entitle the two uterine brothers to one third, the husband to one half and the mother to one-sixth of her property, and nothing would be left for the germane brothers who are in the category of *ᶜaṣabah* (residuaries) and take a share only after the *dhawū al-furūḍ* (Qur'ānic sharers) have taken theirs. The case was brought to the attention of the Caliph, who ruled by way of *istiḥsān* that the germane brothers should share the one-third with the uterine brothers. This was deemed to be just and equitable and it was supported by ᶜUthmān b. ᶜAffān, Zayd ibn Thābit and followed by Imam Mālik, Imam al-Shāfiᶜī and more recently in the reformist legislation of Egypt and Syria in 1943 and 1953 respectively. It is reported that the Caliph ᶜUmar initially applied the normal rules of inheritance and assigned one third to the uterine brothers only, at which point the germane brothers protested, saying 'suppose that our father were a donkey (*ḥimār*), did we not still have the same mother as the deceased?'—which is why the case is also known as *al-Ḥimāriyyah* (the donkey's case). The Caliph was thus persuaded and entitled all the brothers collectively to take a part of the one-third.[35] It is reported concerning the same case that ᶜAlī ibn Abū Ṭālib, Ibn ᶜAbbās, ᶜAbd Allāh ibn Masᶜūd and a number of other prominent Companions, the Imams Abū Ḥanīfah, Aḥmad ibn Ḥanbal and many others held that the germane brothers, who belong to the class of residuaries, should be excluded and the Qur'ānic order of priorities between the various classes of heirs should be applied strictly. This has

in turn provoked the remark that ʿAlī's solution was based on *qiyās*, which was to apply the normal rules regardless of the result, but that ʿUmar's solution was based on *istiḥsān*. ʿUmar's solution took a comprehensive approach and addressed the basic issue of fairness, whereas ʿAlī's solution, although correct to the letter of the text, was less than satisfactory. ʿUmar's solution was based on the rationale that the germane brothers were equal to the uterine brothers as they shared the same mother with them, even if we ignore the fact that they had a superior tie with the deceased by having the same father, and should therefore be given a share not less than that of the uterine brothers.

(2) Suppose someone appoints an agent (*wakīl*) specifically for the purpose of receiving a loan on his behalf and instructs him to receive it as a lump sum, not in separate instalments. But then the *wakīl* receives it in separate payments and having received the final portion he comes to the principal with what he has received. To apply the normal rules of *fiqh* pertaining to special agency (*wakalah khāṣṣah*), the *wakīl* has not followed the instruction he was given and since he acted contrary to the wishes of the principal, he has not fulfilled the terms of the agency and is not considered a *wakīl*. But by recourse to *istiḥsān* founded in considerations of equity and the removal of hardship, an exception is made to the normal rules of *wakālah* and the debtor is accordingly absolved of any blame—and so is the *wakīl* who is also deemed to have complied with the basic terms of his assignment, which was after all to receive the whole of the loan, and this he did the moment he received the final instalment. Hence the agency is held operative and the principal is bound by the act of the *wakīl*.[36]

(3) A similar example to the one above would be when someone deposits a sum of money or a quantity of goods with another person by which to support his family, but the latter who acts as an agent (*wakīl*) spends out of his own account with the intention to deduct it from the deposit. Now to apply the strict rules of *qiyās* in this case would mean, as the Ḥanafīs have held, that whatever the deposit holder has spent will be counted as an act of charity (*tabarruʿ*) as he has in fact acted independently of the instruction he was given, and should consequently return the original deposit to its owner. The amount he has spent shall be deemed a donation or gift, regardless of whether he had the intention to donate or not. He has no right to claim a refund. This would, however, be somewhat less than equitable and there is a case here for a departure from the normal rules. To apply *istiḥsān* here would mean abandoning the idea of *tabarruʿ* in

favour of clearance of account (*al-maqāsah*) between the two parties. For *tabarruᶜ* was not what the principal party had intended in the first place, and if it is not intended by the deposit holder either, then recourse to *tabarruᶜ* is inequitable and out of place. This ruling of *istiḥsān* also applies to the unauthorised agent (*fuḍūlī*) who makes a payment out of his own money on behalf of another person, without any instruction from him, as payment of maintenance, or repayment of a debt, and similar other financial obligations. Under the normal rules, such payments will be considered donations, but *istiḥsān* entitles the *bona fide fuḍūlī* to reimbursement by the beneficiary of such payments.[37]

The only exception whereby the payer is entitled to a refund, under the normal rules, is when he had been coerced into making the payment. One such case is that of a loan borrowed for mortgaging (*mas'alat al-mustaᶜār li'l-rahn*). This is when the property of a person is mortgaged with his permission in lieu of a loan secured by another person, and the debtor does not redeem it. In this case the owner of the mortgaged property may redeem it by paying off the debt himself, and claim it from the debtor. He shall not be considered a donor as he needed to redeem his own property.[38]

H. Other Varieties of *Istiḥsān*

This section looks at some of the lesser known varieties of *istiḥsān*, especially in the works of the Mālikī scholars. The Mālikīs have recognised two other varieties of *istiḥsān*, namely *istiḥsān* on account of abandoning a slight infringement of rules (*istiḥsān bi-tark al-yasīr*), and *istiḥsān* on account of disagreement among the *ᶜulamā'* (*istiḥsān bi-murāᶜāt khilāf al-ᶜulamā'*). The first of these validates a slight infringement of the normal rules in order to remove hardship and facilitate the affairs of people, such as the permissibility of a slight fraud (*al-ghabn al-yasīr*) in transactions, which is tolerated, as is slight *ribā*, such as may be the case in the exchange of a worn out dirham (silver coin) for a new dirham, which may differ a little in weight. This would normally be forbidden under the rules of *ribā* but is tolerated by way of *istiḥsān*. A slight violation of this kind is of no consequence and is as good as none (*fī ḥukm al-ᶜadam*) if it helps remove hardship. Imam Mālik has also allowed hiring a labourer in exchange for his food without specifying the amount he might eat, and also slight amounts of uncertainty and risk-taking (*al-gharar*) in transactions. It is thus permitted to buy or sell a commodity to be delivered 'at the harvest time' even if the precise day is not specified. Imam Mālik did not allow the same degree of latitude in the determination of price and it would therefore vitiate the sale if one were to purchase something say for a dirham or thereabout. On a similar note, the Ḥanafīs have validated the borrowing of loaves of bread by number among neighbours, even though the loaves may differ in weight; the difference is ignored on the basis of *istiḥsān* since it involves tiny quantities and some slight indulgence in *ribā*; yet it is justified by people's need for it.[39]

As for adopting the easiest alternative in matters about which the *ʿulamāʾ* might have disagreed, it represents, according to al-Shāṭibī, one of the recognised varieties of *istiḥsān* in the Mālikī school. There may be two views concerning an issue, one of which is considered preferable (*rājih*), and the other less preferable (*marjūh*). But at times, when the preferred view is actually applied, the implications are such that harm or mischief is created and it consequently outweighs the benefit that made the ruling in question preferable in the first place. Faced with this situation, the jurist tries to prevent the harm by abandoning the preferred ruling in favour of the one which might normally be seen as inferior. The authority for this variety of *istiḥsān* is the *Sunnah* of the Prophet, who was on many occasions annoyed and abused by the enemies of Islam and also by the hypocrites among his own followers, yet he did not act against them for the fear that people might say that 'Muḥammad kills his own Companions.' The Prophet thus acted on the less preferable of the two courses in order to prevent the greater mischief he apprehended.[40] The preferred course would have been to take adequate measures against abuse but the Prophet chose the less preferable alternative of not taking any punitive measures against the agents of this abuse. The word 'kill' in this ḥadīth might have been used for emphasis, in which case it includes punishment other than killing.

A slightly different illustration of the same variety of Mālikī *istiḥsān* is as follows: When an adult woman concludes her own marriage contract without the consent of her guardian (*walī*), then this is a source of disagreement between the Ḥanafī and Mālikī schools. While the Ḥanafīs validate the marriage, it is invalid according to Imam Mālik, but once the marriage has actually been consummated, the Imam nevertheless entitles the woman to dower and inheritance because otherwise the harm that is likely to arise from the application of the preferred view is likely to be greater than the benefit on which this view has actually been premised.[41] To apply the preferred view of the Mālikī school would have the dire consequences of depriving the woman from dower and inheritance, and the offspring of the marriage would also be considered illegitimate. The less preferred view here would be for the Mālikī school to apply the Ḥanafī ruling, which gives partial recognition to the marriage and also entitles the woman to certain rights. There is thus a departure from one view to another, but unlike the usual scenario of *istiḥsān* in which the departure is to a preferable view, in the present case the departure is to a less preferable view; yet it still qualifies as a variety of *istiḥsān*.

Another similar example of *istiḥsān* that selects the less preferable of two alternatives is Imam Mālik's renowned approval of the leadership of the less qualified of two candidates (*Imāma al-mafḍūl*). In the event where one of two candidates for *Imāma* is better qualified than the other but for circumstantial reasons the choice falls nevertheless on the lesser qualified person then the lesser qualified (*al-mafḍūl*) may be elected to be the leader. This could be because the best qualified (*al-afḍal*) was an eminently learned person and a *mujtahid* but the lesser qualified had different skills which were in demand under the prevailing conditions in the community. In such a case the latter may be elected in preference to the better qualified candidate. This represents a departure from what would normally be preferable, which is to elect the best qualified candidate for leadership.

And lastly, in the discussion of the varieties of *istiḥsān* one may briefly include the following classification by the Mālikī jurist Ibn al-Ḥājib (d. 646 AH), who divided *istiḥsān* into the three categories of accepted (*maqbūl*), rejected (*mardūd*) and uncertain (*mutaradad*). The accepted variety includes the following:

(a) Departure from a weaker *qiyās* in favour of a stronger *qiyās*;

(b) Particularisation of a weaker *qiyās* by a stronger *qiyās*;

(c) Departure from an established rule of law to an alternative ruling on the basis of stronger evidence; and

(d) Departure from an established law in favour of custom on the basis of public interest, such as paying a fixed fee for entry to a public bath without specifying the amount of water to be used.

All these instances of *istiḥsān* are covered either by textual sources, consensus or analogy and scholars are on the whole in agreement about them. *Istiḥsān* that does not derive support from any of the recognised proofs, namely textual proofs, consensus or analogy, belongs to the rejected category. And lastly *istiḥsān* of which the jurist himself is not convinced belongs to the uncertain category. Some Ḥanafīs have, for instance, defined *istiḥsān* as 'evidence (*dalīl*) which occurs to the mind of the *mujtahid* but he is unable to articulate it in words'. Ibn al-Ḥājib criticised this and commented that if the jurist is convinced of the strength of that evidence, he may act upon it, in which case his inability to articulate his thoughts is immaterial. In the event, however, when the jurist is indecisive and doubtful as to the strength and validity of *istiḥsān*, it should be resolutely rejected. This is the sort of *istiḥsān* which Ibn al-Ḥājib has classified as disputable (*murtadad*), and he has rightly stated that juristic rulings should be founded on certainty, not indecision and doubt.[42]

I. Ḥanafī and Mālikī Approaches Compared

Comparing the Ḥanafī and Mālikī approaches to *istiḥsān*, one notes that the Mālikī *istiḥsān* derives much of its substance from *maṣlaḥah* and the removal of hardship (*rafʿ al-ḥaraj*). The Ḥanafī *istiḥsān* is on the other hand founded largely on necessity (*ḍarūrah*). The two approaches often yield the same results, however. They differ mainly in regard to the degree of prominence the two schools attach to *maṣlaḥah*. For the Mālikīs, *maṣlaḥah* is a proof in its own right, but the Ḥanafīs do not give it the same degree of prominence. The Mālikīs are inclined to resort to *istiḥsān* in the event of a conflict arising between *qiyās* and *maṣlaḥah*, whereas Ḥanafīs resort to *istiḥsān* in the event of conflict between an obvious *qiyās* and other evidences, especially a stronger *qiyās* and necessity (*ḍarūrah*).[43] These may be said to be the main scholastic tendencies of the Mālikī and Ḥanafī schools concerning *istiḥsān*. But on a general note, the two schools validate *istiḥsān* on these and other grounds including custom, removal of hardship and considerations of equity and fairness. In both schools, *istiḥsān* is concerned, first and foremost, with rectifying the irregularities of *qiyās* (both in its technical sense and in the sense of a normal principle) and the rigidity that is encountered by its strict application in particular cases. Both Ḥanafīs and Mālikīs have turned to *istiḥsān* in order to remedy the rigidities of *qiyās* whenever a ruling of *qiyās* stood in the way of a practical benefit. But the Mālikīs have travelled on this route even further than the Ḥanafīs. This is partly because the Mālikīs took a more open approach to *istiḥsān* in that they have not tied it up with *qiyās* as much as the Ḥanafīs have done. The Mālikīs do not even designate hidden analogy (*al-qiyās al-khafī*) as *istiḥsān* as the Ḥanafīs do. It is rather *qiyās* retaining its original name. For the Mālikīs, *istiḥsān* means departure from an apparent analogy (*qiyās al-ẓāhir*) for any of the following three reasons: (a) when it is in conflict with a predominant and widespread custom; (b) when it clashes with a benefit (*maṣlaḥah*); and (c) when it leads to rigidity and hardship. All of these boil down to *maṣlaḥah*. The Mālikī *istiḥsān*, in other words, is a branch of *maṣlaḥah* that is resorted to in order to remedy the irregularities of *qiyās*.

A ruling of *istiḥsān*, according to the Mālikīs, is also tantamount to giving preference to *maṣlaḥah*, in a particular case, over the ruling of *qiyās*. This is because the textual injunctions of *Sharīᶜah* are generally predicated on the realisation of *maṣlaḥah* and the avoidance and removal of hardship.[44] The Mālikī position here is characterised by Ibn Rushd who wrote that '*istiḥsān* in most cases means paying attention to considerations of public welfare and justice.'[45] This characterisation has, in turn, led al-Zarqā to comment that 'this, in reality corresponds with the necessity-based *istiḥsān* of the Ḥanafī school.'[46] Al-Zarqā went on to compare the Ḥanafī and Shāfiᶜī approaches to *istiḥsān* and to a path one end of which is *istiḥsān* and the other *istiṣlāḥ*. The Ḥanafīs entered this path from the gateway of *istiḥsān* and proceeded to *istiṣlāḥ*, whereas the Mālikīs did the reverse. Each school became famous for the path it chose and the gate by which it entered.[47] The essence of the Ḥanafī *istiḥsān* of necessity is the removal of hardship, and the removal of hardship also strikes a strong note with *maṣlaḥah*. When one compares the two main types of *istiḥsān*, namely the analogical and the exceptional, one notes that *istiḥsān* based on textual sources, consensus and necessity is not extendible to parallel cases. This is because these varieties of *istiḥsān* are not based on particular causes (*ᶜilal*); they are exceptional cases and as such they do not provide a proper basis for analogy. Analogical reasoning (*qiyās*) is primarily concerned with extending the normal, not the exceptional, rules of *Sharīᶜah* to similar cases. But *istiḥsān* founded on latent or hidden analogy (*qiyās khafī*) is extendible, by further analogy, to parallel cases. This may be illustrated as follows: When a dispute arises between a buyer and seller about a price at a time when the buyer has not yet taken delivery, the buyer's version shall be admissible according to *qiyās*. This is because the buyer is likely to be denying the seller's claim for a higher price, and the normal rules of *fiqh* require that one who denies the claim may be asked to take an oath. But according to *istiḥsān*, both parties will be required to take an oath as they each, in a sense, deny the claim of the other; the seller too denies a claim. When both parties have taken such an oath, the transaction shall be nullified. This principle of mutual oath-taking (*taḥāluf*) is then held to be applicable by analogy to the parallel cases of lease and hire (*ijārah*), marriage (*nikāh*) and possible disputes between the heirs of buyers and sellers about prices prior to delivery.[48]

J. A Critique of the Typology *of Istiḥsān*

The existing classification of *istiḥsān*, especially in its Ḥanafī varieties, is not altogether devoid of weakness and this can be seen in regard to *istiḥsān* that consists of discarding an analogy in favour of a ruling of the text or *ijmāʿ*. The basic issue here is whether an *istiḥsān* founded on the authority of the Qur'ān, *Sunnah* or *ijmāʿ* should be called *istiḥsān* at all. In the event where a ḥadīth rules upon something which happens to be contrary to an existing *qiyās*, or represents a departure from the normal rules, then all that one needs in order to authorise the departure in question is the ḥadīth itself. It would, therefore, seem redundant to apply the word '*istiḥsān*' to this form of departure from the rulings of *qiyās*. Whenever a ruling can be found in the Qur'ān or *Sunnah*, the jurist has to follow it and should not have the choice to resort to *qiyās* or to *istiḥsān*. If the Qur'ān provides the choice of an alternative ruling that seems preferable, then the alternative in question is still a Qur'ānic rule, not *istiḥsān*.

The substance of our critique here relates to what al-Ghazālī observed concerning the Ḥanafī *istiḥsān* when he wrote that the jurists of the Shāfiʿī school recognise the validity of *istiḥsān* that is based on the indications of the Qur'ān or *Sunnah*. When there exists evidence of this kind then the case at hand will be governed not by *istiḥsān* but by the provisions of the Qur'ān or *Sunnah* directly. Based on this analysis, al-Ghazālī's critique of *istiḥsān* is not aimed at the analogical *istiḥsān* of the Ḥanafīs, which relate to compulsive necessity or *ḍarūrah*. On the contrary, he has affirmed the latter, since there is no room for doubt therein, but he subsumes it under *qiyās* because the Qur'ān provides direct authority on *ḍarūrah*. Al-Ghazālī has also criticised *istiḥsān* based on custom and has in this context referred to the oft-quoted example of entry to the public bath for a fixed price without quantifying the consumption of water and then raised the question 'how is it known that the community adopted this practice by virtue of *istiḥsān*?' Is it not true, al-Ghazālī added, that this was the custom during the time of the Prophet, in which case it become a tacitly approved *Sunnah* (*Sunnah taqrīriyyah*)?[49]

Al-Zarqā has clearly taken a similar view to that of al-Ghazālī when he wrote that in the presence of a ruling from any of the three superior proofs, namely, the Qur'ān, *Sunnah* and *ijmāᶜ*, there is no room for either *qiyās* or *istiḥsān*. Hence to apply the term *istiḥsān* to such rulings is tantamount to 'forcing something into a category to which it does not belong,' and expatiating over the scope of *istiḥsān* in this way gives rise to uncertainty and confusion.[50] Al-Zarqā continues his critique by drawing a distinction between *Istiḥsān al-Shāriᶜ*, and *Istiḥsān al-faqīh* or the *istiḥsān* of the Lawgiver, and the *istiḥsān* of the jurist respectively.

When a command or a provision is conveyed in a clear text, which diverges from *qiyās* in parallel cases, on account of a *maṣlaḥah* that the Lawgiver has considered in issuing the command, this is the *istiḥsān* of the Lawgiver and that leaves no room for further discussion. We are concerned here only with the *istiḥsān* that is attempted by the jurist, who is engaged in the process of making inferences and deductions from the Lawgiver's injunctions, and resorts to *qiyās* or *istiḥsān* in accordance therewith, getting inspiration from the purposes of the Lawgiver and the objectives of *Sharīᶜah*. The difference between these two types of *istiḥsān*, Zarqā adds, bears some resemblance to the difference, in modern law, between the two types of indicators (*al-qarā'in*), namely statutory indicators, and judicial indicators (*al-qarā'in al-qānūniyyah, al-qarā'in al-qaḍā'iyyah*) respectively. The former are specified by the lawmaker, from which he derives a specific rule, and there is no room for the judge to intervene and interpret. An example of this is the statutory time limit for the hearing of claims (i.e. *al-taqādum*) which the judge has the duty to enforce. Judicial indicators, on the other hand, are those in which the judge has the discretion to evaluate specific disputes. The two are clearly very different. The former provide normative guidelines, whereas the latter belong to the realm of judicial examination and evidence.[51]

Al-Zarqā's analysis finds support in that of al-Shāṭibī, who has tersely stated that *istiḥsān* either relies on revelation or on reason (*al-sharᶜ aw al-ᶜaql*). As for the former 'its preference or denunciation—*istiḥsānuh wa istiqbāhuh*—are clearly known.' When there is a command of the *Sharīᶜah* in regard to doing something, it is presumed to be good and preferable, just as the prohibitions of *Sharīᶜah* which are abominable must be shunned. Thus the Lawgiver does not issue a command unless it is good, and does not forbid anything unless it is reprehensible, and there is no reason to call this *istiḥsān*. There thus remains only one variety of *istiḥsān*, namely *istiḥsān* based on reason. If there is evidence in which a rational *istiḥsān* (*istiḥsān al-ᶜaql*) can find support, it may be identified with this evidence and known as such. Should there be no such evidential support available, then this *istiḥsān* will be akin to a preferable innovation (*bidᶜah mustaḥsanah*) based on the reason and preference of the *mujtahid*, and judgment may be passed in its favour when it is not in conflict with the *Sharīᶜah*. But the concept of *bidᶜah*, al-Shāṭibī adds, applies mainly to matters of worship and the rituals of *ᶜibādāt* for which no evidence can be found in the *Sharīᶜah*.[52]

There may be instances of innovation (*bidᶜa*) in the works of *fiqh* which have been conveniently subsumed under the umbrella of *istiḥsān*. A case is cited, for example, of a woman who was permitted to borrow money in the name of her absent husband. The normal rules would not allow this, but it was said to be permitted by way of *istiḥsān* in the works of latter-day jurists (*muta'akhkhirūn*) including Khayr al-Dīn al-Ramlī. If it is a question of necessity, the case may represent a situation of *istiḥsān* based on necessity, but it would otherwise be a juristic innovation that gained acceptance to allow a wife to borrow in the name of her absent husband. Al-Ramlī has also given some examples of what he calls as *bidᶜa mubāḥa*, or permissible innovation, which has no basis in precedent. To illustrate this would help to clarify the difference between *bidᶜa* and *istiḥsān*. Al-Ramlī refers to a certain custom of the descendants of the Prophet to wear green turbans and carry green flags in processions. Ramlī responds that these customs are not mentioned in the classical sources and fall therefore under permissible innovation. The opposite of this is the negative innovation (*bidᶜa qabīḥa*) which is illustrated in a practice in Ottoman Turkey where the master artisans of a guild in a town assembled whenever a new member sought permission to join the profession. The candidate was required to feed the entire gathering of the guild, at great cost and hardship, without any basis for this in the law. This was a pernicious custom and a *bidᶜa* that had nothing to do with *istiḥsān*, and any attempt to bring such practices into the ambit of *istiḥsān* would be to no avail. The enormity of the guild practice in the case just reviewed is also manifested in the unwarranted restriction it imposes on the individual's freedom of movement and work.[53]

The present review of the typology of *istiḥsān* shows some of the varieties in the conventional classifications of *istihsān* to be redundant, yet one also finds that the conventional classification of istiḥsān is not exhaustive, as one comes across instances of *istiḥsān* that do not fit under any of the existing varieties. For instance, *istiḥsān* based on equity and the consideration of fairness has not been given a separate entry in the scholastic treatment of *istiḥsān* by either the Ḥanafīs or Mālikīs. Instances of equitable *istiḥsān* often seem to have been subsumed under considerations of *rafᶜ al-ḥaraj*. The removal of hardship is admittedly the nearest concept to that of equity and fairness, and as it has a definitive Qur'ānic identity and provides an eminently suitable basis for *istiḥsān*. Yet it is ironic that neither of these (i.e. equity and *rafᶜ al-ḥaraj*) find a separate entry in the scholastic typology of *istiḥsān*. It seems that the *maṣlaḥah*-based *istiḥsān* has a strong base of identity with *rafᶜ al-ḥaraj* and the *ᶜulamā'* do tend to almost equate one with the other. This can also be said of custom, which is recognised as a proof precisely because acting on custom is in the spirit of *rafᶜ al-ḥaraj*. But when both *maṣlaḥah* and custom are recognised as separate bases of *istiḥsān*, the question naturally arises as to whether one should add *rafᶜ al-ḥaraj* and also equity and fairness (*iḥsān*) to the existing varieties of *istiḥsān*.

As I discussed earlier, the basic notion of equity, especially the way it has been treated in Western jurisprudence, may be less than acceptable to Muslim jurists. This may partially explain why one does not find an equity-based *istiḥsān* separately identified in the works of the *ᶜulamā'*. One may add here that the Mālikī characterisation of *istiḥsān* as 'acting on the stronger of two evidences' is perhaps comprehensive enough to leave open the possibility of adding new types of *istiḥsān* to those that have been identified so far. One might on the other hand think that the Mālikī definition in a sense makes the whole idea of the classification of *istiḥsān* into specific types redundant: When it is said that *istiḥsān* is acting on the stronger of two evidences or proofs, the evidence in question may be any recognised and valid evidence. At this juncture one is reminded of the hazards of perceiving too many types and categories of *istiḥsān*, since in certain instances of its application one may find that more than one type of *istiḥsān* can be identified in reference to the same issue. One can imagine, for instance, that *istiḥsān* supported by general custom may simultaneously be classified under necessity and *maṣlaḥah*. Be that as it may, it seems that both Mālikī and Ḥanafī *ᶜulamā'* have adopted the basic approach of identifying the evidential grounding of *istiḥsān*, and that approach is, in the final analysis, preferable to leaving the scope of *istiḥsān* wide open by merely saying, for instance, that *istiḥsān* is acting on the stronger of two indications. The correct approach with regard to a controversial idea such as *istiḥsān* is therefore not the generic approach but one which looks at the particulars and produces evidence at every step, as it were. My attempt to propose the two additional types of *istiḥsān* based on *raf^c al-ḥaraj* and considerations of equity and fairness (*iḥsān*) aims to be in conformity with this approach.

The basic notion of *iḥsān* side by side with justice (*^cadl*) finds ample support in the Qur'ān. It is also interesting to find a certain juxtaposition between these two concepts in the Qur'ān, when one reads, for example, that 'God commands justice (*^cadl*), the doing of good (*iḥsān*) and liberality to kith and kin...' (al-Nahl, 16:90). The main difference between justice and *iḥsān* may be said to be that justice is the normal requirement to be administered under the *Sharī^cah*. *Iḥsān* on the other hand opens up the scope of justice under positive law to considerations of equity and good conscience, especially in the event where the application of normal rules may not actually secure justice, in which case one should act in the spirit of *iḥsān* and find a method that serves the ideals of Qur'ānic justice, even if this entails a certain departure from specific rules. In the examples, cited earlier, the case of *Mushtaraka*, which became a subject of debate among the Companions, was a typical case of equity-based *istiḥsān*. It was a case of *istiḥsān* that proceeded on the Qur'ānic notion of *iḥsān* (fair dealing). On a similar note, cases involving the removal of hardship (*raf^c al-ḥaraj*) have often been subsumed under the category of necessity-based *istiḥsān*. Yet there is a conceptional difference between *ḍarūrah* (necessity) and *raf^c al-ḥaraj* (removal of hardship), as the latter can be attempted in cases that may be less pressing than those of absolute necessity, and the two can therefore be separate types of *istiḥsān*.

NOTES

1. Sarakhsī, *Uṣūl*, II, 203.
2. Cf. Sha^cbān, *Uṣūl*, p. 153; Khallāf, *^cIlm Uṣūl al-Fiqh*. 12th edn, Kuwait, Dār al-Qalam, 1398/1978, p. 82.
3. Cf. Al-Zarqā, *Al-Istiṣlāḥ wa Masālih al-Mursalah fi'l-Sharī^cah al-Islāmiyyah*. Damascus, Dār al-Qalam, 1408/1988, p. 24; Al-Nabhānī, *Muqaddimah al-Dustūr*. Beirut, n.p., 1967, p. 67.
4. Ibn ^cĀbidin, *Ḥāshiyah Radd al-Mukhtār ^cala Durr al-Mukhtār*. Cairo, Dār al-Fikr, 1399/1979, IV, 413; Zarqā, *Al-Madkhal*, I, 79–80.
5. Cf. Al-Zarqā, *Al-*Istiṣlāḥ, p. 25; Idem, *Al-Madkhal*, I, 80; ^cUmar al-Dīn, Muḥammad. 'Istiḥsān and Masalih-e Mursalah,' in *Al-Majlis al-A^cla li-Ri^cāyat al-Funun wa'l-Adab wa'l-^cUlūm al-Ijtima^ciyyah, Usbu^c al-Fiqh al-Islāmī wa Mihrajān al-Imām Ibn Taymiyyah*. Damascus: n.p., 1380/1960, p. 349.
6. Sha^cbān, *Uṣūl*, pp. 153–154; al-Zarqā, *Al-Istiṣlāḥ*, p. 25.
7. Al-Bukhārī, *Ṣaḥīḥ al-Bukhārī*. Eng. Trans. Muḥammad Muḥsin Khān, Lahore, Kazi Publications, 1979, III, 243, ḥadīth No. 441.

8. Abū Dāwūd, *Sunan Abū Dāwūd*. Eng. trans. Aḥmad Ḥasan, 3 vols, Lahore, Ashraf Press, 1984, *K. al-Buyuᶜ, b. fī Bayᶜ al-Rajul ma Laysa ᶜIndah.*

9. Cf. Zarqā, *Al-Madkhal*, I, 85.

10. Cf. Shaᶜbān, *Uṣūl*, p. 146; *al-Madkhal*, p. 123.

11. Khallāf, *ᶜIlm*, p. 82; Mūsā, *Al-Madkhal li-Dirāsah al-Fiqh al-Islāmī*. 2nd. edn, Cairo, Dār al-Fikr al-ᶜArabī, 1373/1953, p. 197.

12. Abū Zahrah, *Uṣūl*, p. 211; Al-Zuḥaylī, *Uṣūl*, p. 744.

13. Zarqā, *Al-Madkhal*, I, 85.

14. Al-Shāṭibī, *Muwāfaqāt*, IV, 117.

15. Cf. Mikādi, 'Baḥth fī'l-Istiḥsān', p. 314.

16. Ibn ᶜĀbidin, *Radd al-Mukhtār*, V, 43; Mikādi, 'Baḥth fī'l-Istiḥsān', p. 311.

17. Al-Zaylaᶜī, *Tabyīn al-Ḥaqā'iq Sharḥ Kanz al-Daqā'iq*. Egypt, Būlāq, 1313 AH, III, 65; Ibn al-Humām, *Fatḥ al-Qadīr Sharḥ al-Hidāyah*. Egypt, Būlāq, 1315-1318 AH, III, 354; Maḥmassānī, *Al-Mawjibāt wa'l-ᶜUqūd fī'l-Sharīᶜah al-Islāmiyyah*, 3rd edn. Beirut, Dār al-ᶜIlm li'l-Malāyīn, 1983, I, 76; Mikādi, 'Baḥth fī'l-Istiḥsān', p. 327.

18. Ibn Qayyim al-Jawziyyah, *Iᶜlām al-Muwaqqiᶜīn ᶜan Rabb al-ᶜĀlāmin*, ed. Muḥammad Munīr al-Dimashqī. Cairo, Idārah al-Ṭībāᶜah al-Munīriyyah, 4 vols., n.d., III, 18; Mikādi, 'Baḥth fī'l-Istiḥsān', p. 327.

19. Al-Zaylaᶜī, *Sharḥ al-Kanz*, III, 65.

20. Ibn ᶜĀbidin, *Radd al-Mukhtār*, V, 175; Maḥmassānī, *Al-Mawjibāt*, I, 77.

21. Ibn Qayyim, *al-Ṭuruq al-Ḥukmiyyah fī'l-Siyāsah al-Sharīᶜiyyah*. Cairo, Mu'assasah al-ᶜArabiyyah li'l-Ṭībāᶜah, 1380/1961, pp. 23-24 and 157; al-Shawkānī, *Nayl al-Awṭār Sharḥ Muntaqā al-Akhbār*. Cairo, Muṣṭafā al-Bābī al-Ḥalabī, n.d., IX, 204; Mikādi, 'Baḥth fī'l-Istiḥsān', p. 308.

22. Gerber, 'Rigidity Versus Openness,' p. 191, referring to al-Ramli's *al-Fatāwā al-Khayriyya*, II, 203.

23. Al-Shāṭibī, *Muwāfaqāt*, IV, 117.

24. Abū Sulaymān, *Al-Fikr al Uṣūli*, p. 222; Abū Zahrah, *Mālik: Ḥayātuh wa ᶜAṣruh, Arā'uh wa Fiqhuh*. 2nd edn. Cairo, Dār al-Fikr al-ᶜArabī, 1952, para 218; Zarqā, *Al-Madkhal*, I, 82.

25. Cf. Zaydān, *Al-Wajīz*, p.232.

26. Mikādi, 'Baḥth fī'l-Istiḥsān', p.327.

27. Cf. Qādi Simawnah, *Jāmiᶜ al-Fusulayn*. Cairo, Maṭbaᶜah al-Amiriyyah, 1300 AH, II, 272; Mikādi, 'Baḥth fī'l-Istiḥsān', p.328.

28. Cf. Shaᶜbān, *Uṣūl*, p. 151.

29. See generally the IRTI Seminar Proceedings on *Waqf* related issues entitled *Management and Development of Awqaf*. Jeddah (Saudi Arabia), 1407/1987.

30. Cf. Al-Shāṭibī, *al-Iᶜtiṣām*, II, 318, al-Mashāt, *Al-Jawāhir*, p. 220.

31. Shaᶜbān, *Uṣūl*, p. 151.

32. Cf. Al-Husari, *Al-Dawlah wa Siyāsat al-Ḥukm*, p. 87.

33. Ibn ᶜĀbidin, *Ḥāshiyah Radd al-Mukhtār*, III, 98; Mikādi, 'Baḥth fī'l-Istiḥsān', p. 313.

34. Al-Āmidī, *Iḥkām*, IV, 156.

35. Ibn Rushd, *Bidāyah*, II, 290; Zarqā, *Al-Madkhal*, I, 87.

36. Ibn ᶜĀbidin, *Ḥāshiyah Radd al-Mukhtār*, III, 515.

37. Ibn ʿĀbidin, *Ḥāshiyah Radd al-Mukhtār*, IV, 415 (chapter on *Wakālah*); Zarqā, *Al-Istiṣlāḥ*, p. 28; idem., *Al-Madkhal*, I, 83.
38. Ibn ʿĀbidin, *Ḥāshiyah Radd al-Mukhtār*, V, 331; Zarqā, *Al-Madkhal*, I, 83.
39. Ibn ʿĀbidin, *Ḥāshiyah Radd al-Mukhtār*, IV, 172; Zarqā, *Al-Madkhal*, I, 83; Mīqā, *Al-Ra'y*, p. 430.
40. Al-Shāṭibī, *Al-Iʿtiṣām*, II, 145; al-Mashāt, *Al-Jawāhir*, p. 202.
41. Al-Shāṭibī, *Muwāfaqāt*, IV, 202; Mīqā, *Al-Ra'y*, 432.
42. Ibn al-Ḥājib, *Mukhtaṣar al-Muntahā'*. Constantinople, al-Maktabah al-Islāmiyyah, 1310 AH, II, 458; Aḥmad Ḥasan, *Analogical Reasoning*, p. 419.
43. Cf. Abū Zahrah, 'Taʿliq', p. 363; Mikādi, 'Baḥth fī'l-Istiḥsān', p. 315.
44. Zarqā, *Al-Madkhal*, I, 87-88.
45. Ibn Rushd, *Bidāyah*, II, 154; see also Zarqā, *Al-Madkhal*, I, 88.
46. Zarqā, *Al-Madkhal*, I, 88.
47. Ibid., I, 121.
48. Sarakhsī, *Uṣūl*, II, 206; *Taftāzānī*, *Talwīḥ*, II, 83: Aḥmad Ḥasan, *Analogical Reasoning*, p. 417–418.
49. Al-Ghazālī, *Mustaṣfā*, II, 138.
50. Zarqā, *Al-Madkhal*, I, 86.
51. Ibid., I, 86-87.
52. Al-Shāṭibī, *al-Iʿtiṣām*, II, 138.
53. Cf. al-Ramlī, *Al-Fatāwā al-Kubrā al-Fiqhiyya*. 4 vols. Egypt: Būlāq, 1308 AH. II, 235, also discussed by Gerber 'Rigidity Versus Openness', p. 192.

CHAPTER FIVE

Proof *(Ḥujjiyyah)* of Istiḥsān

Ḥanafī jurists have quoted the following Qur'ānic passages in support of *istiḥsān*.

(1) So give good tidings to My servants who listen to the word, then follow the best of it. (al-Zumar, 39: 17–18)

فبشر عبادِ الّذين يستمعون القول فيتبعون أحسنه

(2) And follow the best of what has been sent down to you from your Lord. (al-Zumar, 39: 55)

واتبعوا أحسن ما أنزل إليكم من ربكم

(3) In another place, the Qur'ān recounts that God instructed Prophet Moses to 'enjoin your people to hold fast by the best in the precepts'. (al-Aʿrāf, 7:145)

وأمر قومك يأخذوا بأحسنها

The reference in this last verse is to the Tablets (*al-alwāḥ*) which contained the essential spiritual truth, from which positive injunctions, explanations and interpretations were derived. These precepts contained matters absolutely forbidden, matters not forbidden but disapproved, and matters about which there was no prohibition or injunction. No soul was to be burdened beyond its capacity but people were asked to seek the best and highest possible conduct.[1]

To follow the best speech and evidence, the central message of these *āyāt*, is also the essence of *istiḥsān*. *Istiḥsān* involves abandoning weaker evidence in favour of stronger evidence which is in greater harmony with the goals of *Sharīʿah*, and the Qur'ān clearly validates this.

According to al-Sarakhsī, listening to the words of God Most High and following the best of it can mean two things to a jurist. Firstly, to exert oneself by way of *ijtihād* and the best that *ra'y* can achieve in understanding those parts of the Qur'ān which have been left open to the exercise of *ra'y*. This is the case for example with regard to determining the quantity of the gift of consolation (*mutʿah*) which the Qur'ān has not specified but about which it has said 'a fair gift is due from those who wish to do what is right' (al-Baqarah, 2: 236). *Mutʿah* should therefore be determined in line with the financial capability and means at one's disposal, provided that it accords with the Qur'ānic stipulation of *bi'l-maʿrūf* (fair, equitable). What is required in this verse, al-Sarakhsī added, is to exercise one's best judgement based on the predominance of *ra'y*, which is what is involved in *istiḥsān*. In another place the Qur'ān lays down the obligation that a father provide for the maintenance and clothing of his children in a manner that is decent and fair (*bi'l-maʿrūf*) (al-Baqarah, 2:233). But once again the text here does not specify any quantities. There is little doubt, al-Sarakhsī added, about the substance of this kind of *istiḥsān*, and the jurists are generally in agreement with it. This is, in fact, one of the two main types of *istiḥsān* that al-Jassās (d. 370 AH) earlier identified as the determination of the quantitative aspects of textual rulings which the *mujtahid* attempts (*ithbāt al-maqādīr al-mawkulah ilā ijtihādinā*). The other type of *istiḥsān* al-Jassās has discussed is concerned with the abandonment of *qiyās* for an alternative ruling that is deemed preferable.[2] Secondly, 'to listen to the word and follow the best of it,' al-Sarakhsī wrote, could also be understood with reference to the underlying proof of *qiyās*. The proof (*dalīl*) which conflicts with an obvious *qiyās* is superseded by that *qiyās*, but is then re-discovered after consideration and deeper thought, and it then emerges a stronger evidence and provides for a better understanding of the *Sharīʿah* and a preferable course of action. This is what lies at the centre of the juristic *istiḥsān*, that is, the intellectual effort to distinguish between the stronger evidence and that which is merely plausible in reference to a particular *ḥukm*.[3]

A similar but different understanding of the same Qur'ānic passages is conveyed in Yusuf Ali's commentary, to the effect that the reference here is to a higher or superior course of conduct. The Qur'ān has, in others words, distinguished a preferable course of conduct from that which may be considered ordinary. Punishing the wrongdoer, for example, is a normal process enjoined by the *Sharīᶜah*, but forgiving him or her may at times be preferable (*aḥsan*) and would thus represent the higher course of conduct.[4]

The following statement of ᶜAbd Allāh b. Masᶜūd, often identified as an elevated (*marfūᶜ*) ḥadīth, is commonly quoted in support of *istiḥsān*: 'What the Muslims deem to be good is good in the sight of God.'[5]

ما رآه المسلمون حسنا فهو عند الله حسن

The essence of *istiḥsān* in almost all its varieties is encapsulated in another ḥadīth which states that: 'harm is neither inflicted nor reciprocated in Islam.'[6]

لا ضرر ولا ضرار في الإسلام

The essence of *istiḥsān* is to prevent harm and alleviate hardship. While this is the general goal and spirit of *Sharīᶜah*, *istiḥsān* provides a methodology and evidential basis for its application and translates that general message into a workable formula. The need for this is evident when one is reminded of the fact that the goals of *Sharīᶜah* are numerous, and it is often a question of ascertaining an order of priority or preference in values – and this is what *istiḥsān* is fundamentally designed to achieve.

Frequent instances of *istiḥsān* in the sense of making exceptions to normal rules can be found in the Qur'ān and *Sunnah*. For example, the Qur'ān lays down the duty of fasting in Ramadan but at the same time makes exceptions for those who are sick or travelling (al-Baqarah, 2:185). Elsewhere, one finds that the Qur'ān spells out a number of prohibitions concerning certain varieties of food which are then followed by an exception generally granted to 'whoever is compelled by hunger, not inclining willfully to sin, then surely God is Forgiving, Merciful.' (al-Mā'idah, 5:3). Similarly, the *Sunnah* lays down the rules of *ribā'* pertaining to certain commodities and then makes an exception to permit what is known as *ᶜarāyā*, that is sale of wet dates on the tree in exchange for dry dates, because of people's need for this. The Companions too have acted in line with the spirit of the Qur'ān and *Sunnah* and made exceptions to general rules on grounds of equity and the removal of hardship. An example of this was the decision of the third Caliph ᶜUthmān to entitle to inheritance a woman who was divorced by her dying husband in order to exclude her from inheritance. The normal rules would have excluded a divorcee from inheritance since divorce breaks the marital tie. But considerations of fairness prompted the Caliph ᶜUthmān and other Companions to exercise *ijtihād* based on *ra'y* and make an exception in this case. The majority of the leading *madhāhib*, namely the Ḥanafīs, Mālikīs and Ḥanbalīs, have maintained the view that the departure from an established ruling to an alternative ruling in *istiḥsān* must have a basis (i.e. *sanad*) in the other recognized proofs of *Sharīᶜah*.[7] It is in other words a variety of *ijtihād* which injects a measure of flexibility into the fabric of the *Sharīᶜah* by making necessary concessions to ensure that technical conformity to specific rules does not frustrate the higher objectives of justice and *maṣlaḥah*.

The critics of *istiḥsān* have argued, however, that none of the foregoing provide a definite authority in support of the doctrine. Regarding the first of the three verses, for example, Āmidī pointed out that it merely praises those who follow the best of what they hear. There is no indication in this *āyah* to render adherence to the 'best speech' an obligation. Nor does the second *āyah* bind one to search for the best in the revelation: if there is an injunction in the revealed sources, it would bind the individual regardless of whether it is the best of the revelation or otherwise.[8] As for the Tradition, 'what the Muslims deem good is good in the sight of God', both al-Ghazālī and al-Āmidi have observed that, if anything, this provides the authority for the basic validity of consensus (*ijmāᶜ*). There is nothing in this Tradition to suggest, and indeed it would be arbitary to say, that what a Muslim individual deems good is also good in the sight of God.[9]

The critics of *istiḥsān* have further suggested that this doctrine was initially introduced by Ḥanafī jurists in response to certain urgent situations. The Ḥanafīs then tried to justify themselves by quoting the Qur'ān and the ḥadīth *ex-post facto*. The Qur'ānic foundation of *istiḥsān*, in other words, is weak, and no explicit authority for it can be found in the *Sunnah* either.[10]

The textual evidence quoted in support of *istiḥsān* is admittedly speculative (*ẓannī*), but then one might say that this is not a peculiarity of *istiḥsān*. To the reader of *uṣūl al-fiqh* who looks into the textual evidence of such other recognized proofs of *Sharīᶜah* as *maṣlaḥah*, or even *ijmāᶜ* and *qiyās*, the general conclusions we have come to here would by no means seem unfamiliar. Much of the textual evidence that is quoted in support of these doctrines is *ẓannī*, although some may be a little more persuasive than others. Like these other doctrines, *istiḥsān* too is primarily a rational, not a textual, proof. But when it is realised that as a rational proof, *istiḥsān* follows the guidance of the text and serves as an instrument for the realisation of its goals and objectives, then its basic validity is not in doubt, even in the absence of a specific text to that effect.

NOTES

1. Cf. *The Holy Qur'ān, Text, Translation and Commentary* by Abdullah Yusuf Ali. Jeddah: Islamic Education Centre, 1984, note 1107.
2. Al-Jassās, *Uṣūl*, p. 296, quoted from the unpublished ms of *Kitāb al-Fuṣūl fi'l-Uṣūl*, p. 296 by Abū Sulayman *Al-Fikr al-Uṣūli*, p. 153.
3. Al-Sarakhsī, *Uṣūl al-Sarakhsī*. Ed. Abu'l-Wafā al-Afghānī. Cairo: Maṭbaᶜah Dār al-Kitāb al-ᶜArabī, 1372 AH, II, 200.
4. Yusuf Ali, *Holy Qur'ān*, n. 4269.
5. Al-Shāṭibī, *al-Iᶜtiṣām*, II, 319; Al-Āmidi, *Iḥkām*, I, 214.
6. Ibn Mājah, *Sunan Ibn Mājah*. Istanbul: Cagri Yaginlari, 2 vols. 1401/1981, II, 784, ḥadīth no. 2340.
7. Cf. Mīqā, *Al-Ra'y*, pp. 393-406.
8. Al-Āmidī, *Iḥkām*, IV, 159.
9. Ibid., IV, 160; al-Ghazālī, *Mustasfa*, I, 138.
10. Cf. Aḥmad Ḥasan, 'The Principle of Istiḥsān,' p. 347.

CHAPTER SIX

The Argument Against *Istiḥsān*

As indicated earlier, *istiḥsān* is basically a Ḥanafī doctrine also upheld by the Mālikī and Ḥanbalī schools, while the Shāfiʿīs, the Ẓāhirīs, the Shīʿah and Muʿtazilah have disputed its basic validity. The argument against the validity of *istiḥsān* is, on the whole, less than convincing, however. Many writers who have looked into the controversy surrounding *istiḥsān* have reached the conclusion that despite the wide-ranging opposition to *istiḥsān* in the scholastic literature of the *madhāhib*, the basic notion of *istiḥsān*, nevertheless, finds support in almost all the *madhāhib*.[1] Imam al-Shāfiʿī's refutation of this doctrine is by far the most explicit as he left no one in doubt when he called the section on *istiḥsān* in his *Kitāb Al-Umm* (vol. VII) '*Kitāb Ibṭāl al-Istiḥsān* (book on the nullification/falsehood of *istiḥsān*').

In his writings both in *Al-Risālah* and *Al-Umm*, Imam al-Shāfiʿī considered *istiḥsān* a form of arbitrary indulgence in personal preferences, which he equated with pleasure-seeking (*taladhudh wa hawā*). For Imam al-Shāfiʿī, a Muslim must obey God and His Messenger at all times and follow the injunctions enshrined in the scripture. Differences of opinion and disputes must be resolved in the light of the guidance of the Qur'ān and *Sunnah*, and he quoted to this effect the Qur'ānic *āyah* in Sura al-Nisā' (4:59) which makes this point. Al-Shāfiʿī wrote that anyone who ruled or gave a *fatwā* on the basis of a *naṣṣ*, or on the basis of *ijtihād* which drew an analogy with the *naṣṣ*, fulfilled his basic duty and complied with correct guidance. But anyone who preferred that which neither God nor His Messenger had recommended would have deviated, and his choice would not be acceptable to either God or the Prophet. Since *istiḥsān* relies on personal opinion, discretion and the preference of the individual jurist, it was not in harmony with the Qur'ānic dictum 'Does man think he has been left without guidance?' (al-Qiyāmah, 75:36).

أيحسب الإنسان أن يترك سدى

Al-Shāfiʿī added: if every judge and every *muftī* ruled according to their own inclinations, one can imagine that self-indulgence and chaos would afflict the life of the community. Unlike *qiyās*, whose propriety can be tested by the methodology it must follow, *istiḥsān* is not regulated as such. Since *istiḥsān* consists neither of *naṣṣ* nor analogy to the *naṣṣ*, it is *ultra vires* and must therefore be avoided.[2] It should be noted here that *istiḥsān* in al-Shāfiʿī's parlance includes what in juristic terminology is known as *al-maṣāliḥ al-mursalah* (unrestricted interest), as well as *istiḥsān* as understood by the Ḥanafis and Mālikīs.[3]

Al-Shāfiʿī further added that the Prophet himself, although divinely inspired in whatever he ruled, was often asked questions about issues, but he did not resort to *istiḥsān*. Instead he would wait for a divine ruling and would follow it whenever it was revealed to him, such as in the cases of *liʿān* and *ẓihār* (two types of divorce to which references are found in the Qur'ān and the *fiqh* literature). Al-Shāfiʿī wrote that the Prophet had in fact denounced instances of *istiḥsān* by the Companions – when he was informed, for example, of the incident when a person was killed by one of the Companions in battle even though he professed Islam, albeit under pain of a sword hanging over his head.[4]

Many scholars both within and outside the Shāfiʿī school have concluded, however, that notwithstanding his vigorous refutation of *istiḥsān*, Imam al-Shāfiʿī himself has resorted to it. Thus it is suggested that on at least five occasions al-Shāfiʿī has had recourse to *istiḥsān*: when he wrote that he preferred the gift of consolation following divorce (*mutʿah*) to be thirty dirhams; he preferred the right of pre-emption to be three days; and he preferred to leave a portion of the payments to a contracted slave (*al-mukātab*) in lieu of his release. He also said he preferred that the Qur'ān should be placed on the lap of one who takes an oath for greater emphasis (*taghlīzan*). And then the fact that al-Shāfiʿī upheld the *istiḥsānī* solution of ʿUmar ibn al-Khaṭṭāb in the well-known inheritance case of *al-mushtarakah* is evidence of his acceptance of *istiḥsān*. On certain other occasions the Imam has used the parallel term *istiḥbāb* (liking or preference) instead of '*istiḥsān*', but for an essentially similar purpose.[5]

Sarakhsī has criticised al-Shāfiʿī's stand on *istiḥsān* and said that the essence of *istiḥsān* is to act on the stronger of two indications, which is far from the pursuit of personal whim and desire. Sarakhsī adds that *istiḥsān* is, in fact, a kind of systematic reasoning like *qiyās*. Al-Shāfiʿī himself maintained, argues Sarakhsī, that various kinds of systematic reasoning can be included under the broad concept of *qiyās*. Then he adds that al-Shāfiʿī often spoke in such terms as *astaḥibbu dhālika* (I like that) which is tantamount to saying *astaḥsinu kadhā* (I prefer such-and-such); they both convey the same purpose, although *astaḥsinu* is more eloquent and closer to the purpose it is supposed to convey. Having analysed al-Shāfiʿī's views on *istiḥsān*, Sarakhsī concluded that what al-Shāfiʿī brought out as objections are in reality not objections.[6]

There is general agreement that if *istiḥsān* were to consist of following personal fancy and desire, as al-Shāfiʿī claimed, then it would fall outside the meaning and purpose that the proponents of *istiḥsān* had intended for the doctrine. No one can be expected to approve that sort of indulgence in arbitrariness. But when *istiḥsān* is seen in its proper perspective, its basic validity and strength as an instrument of flexibility and pragmatism is beyond challenge.

Ibn Taymiyya has also discussed al-Shāfiʿī's views on *istiḥsān* and has drawn attention to the point that al-Shāfiʿī might have taken two different positions on *istiḥsān*, each pertaining to his old and new schools respectively.[7]

Abū Zahrah has made the observation that al-Shāfiʿī's refutation of *istiḥsān* referred only to *istiḥsān* that was founded on *maṣlaḥah*, since elsewhere the Imam has also refuted the idea of *maṣlaḥah* and its authority as a proof of *Sharīʿah*. Al-Shāfiʿī was highly critical of Imam Mālik's epithetical statement that '*istiḥsān* represents nine-tenths of human knowledge'. This characterisation of *istiḥsān* was basically focused on *maṣlaḥah*, and on what later gave rise to the phrase 'al-Istiḥsān al-Mālikī' (Mālikī *istiḥsān)*. It was basically this statement that provoked the equally remarkable statement from al-Shāfiʿī in which he claims that *istiḥsān* is tantamount to pleasure-seeking in religion, tantamount to saying that God has left man without guidance, and that man is free to act on *maṣlaḥah* without evidence. Abū Zahrah went on to say that the *istiḥsān* refuted by al-Shāfiʿī does not really include Ḥanafī *istiḥsān*. This is because Ḥanafī *istiḥsān* does not rely on unrestricted reasoning (*istidlal mursal*), or even on unrestricted *maṣlaḥah*, but consists of a departure from one recognised proof in favour of another, from a weaker evidence to a stronger, more persuasive evidence.[8] According to yet another observer, al-Shāfiʿī's rejection of *istiḥsān* 'should be interpreted as a renunciation of inconsistency in its use in the early period before him'.[9]

It seems that Imam Shāfiʿī's refutation of *istiḥsān* was partially motivated by the desire to champion the cause of the Traditionists (Ahl al-Ḥadīth) and to present a rigorous critique of the views and attitudes of the Rationalists (Ahl al-Ra'y). In this context it is quite possible that the Imam took a somewhat exaggerated view of *istiḥsān* and came out against it rather too strongly perhaps, and equated *istiḥsān* with pleasure seeking and indulgence in unwarranted opinionating.

Ibn Ḥazm al-Ẓāhirī's understanding of *istiḥsān* came close to that of al-Shāfiʿī, which is perhaps what one would expect, bearing in mind the literalist orientations of his *uṣūlī* thought, and the fact that he was initially a follower of the Shāfiʿī school. Ibn Ḥazm highlighted the inconsistencies of reliance on *istiḥsān* and the disconcerting effect it might have on the *Sharīʿah* when he wrote: 'We find that the Ḥanafīs have considered good (*istaḥsanū*) what the Mālikīs have considered reprehensible (*istaqbahū*) and vice versa. Then to rely on the *istiḥsān* of some people, in our search for truth in God's religion, is likely to be in vain'. *Istiḥsān*, according to Ibn Ḥazm, is misguided indulgence in pursuit of desire (*hawā*) that can only lead to disagreement and confusion, and it is in any case essentially objectionable to make personal preference the determinant of truth. Islam is self-contained and complete and there is no room in it for *istiḥsān*. Ibn Ḥazm also refuted the relevance of the oft-quoted statement of ʿAbd Allah Ibn Masʿūd to *istiḥsān* when he (Ibn Ḥazm) said: 'To equate what only some Muslims approve to approval in the sight of God Most High is arbitrary and in any case tantamount to misunderstanding the meaning of Ibn Masʿūd's statement. In saying 'what the Muslims deem to be good is good in the sight of God,' Ibn Masʿūd surely referred to the consensus (*ijmāʿ*) of all the Muslims, not to the *istiḥsān* of some individuals'. Ibn Ḥazm further criticised the link between *istiḥsān* and *qiyās* and the fact that the former is often said to be a more accurate variety of *qiyās*. All that this analogy tells us is that there is some inherent falsehood in *qiyās*: if one *qiyās* necessitates the abandonment of another *qiyās* because they are contradictory to one another then this falsifies *qiyās* as a whole. For one truth neither falsifies nor contradicts another truth and thus both *qiyās* and *istiḥsān* are invalid, according to Ibn Ḥazm. Much of the *istiḥsān* that Abū Ḥanīfah and Mālik upheld refers to customary practices in their times, or to what they considered appropriate under the circumstances. All of this, Ibn Ḥazm adds, was arbitrary and at odds with the Qur'ānic statements: 'and He forbade the self of man from indulgence in desire' and 'the self of man is certainly prone to evil'; and 'who is more misguided than the one who followed his desire away from God's guidance'.[10] Lastly, Ibn Ḥazm quotes the text in Sūra al-Nisā' (4:59) which enjoins the believers to refer their disputes 'to God and His Messenger', not to the *mustahsinūn*, that is the partisans of *istiḥsān*.

The Imāmī Shiᶜah have also rejected *istiḥsān* by virtue of the analysis that it consists either of the subjective inclination and preference of individual jurists without any Sharᶜī proof, or of a departure from a normal rule of *Sharīᶜah* to a customary rule, which is of little validity in *Sharīᶜah*. The Imāmiyyah also argue that with *istiḥsān* consisting of acting upon a valid and recognised custom that if the custom is upheld by the *Sharīᶜah*, this custom itself will provide evidence for its validity, not *istiḥsān* as such. For a custom of this type is equivalent to general consensus, and would be tantamount to acting on *ijmāᶜ* rather than custom. A reference is then made to the oft-cited example of charging a fixed fee for entry to the public bath, which is upheld by *ijmāᶜ*. *Istiḥsān* based only on the personal preference of a *mujtahid* is thus not a proof for the Imāmī Shīᶜah and not a valid basis for *hukm*.[11]

In a response to Ibn Ḥazm's critique, it has been suggested that his refutation of *istiḥsān* and his reference to contradictory analogies is not quite accurate. For the Ḥanafīs have explained that analogy-based *istiḥsān* is not just abandoning one *qiyās* for another but is acting on the stronger of two possible analogies from the start. The process involved is not discarding a *qiyās* that has been upheld and validated and then abandoned; it is rather acting on the stronger of two conceivable analogies. The Ḥanafīs have also held that in the event of a conflict between *istiḥsān* and *qiyās*, preference is to be given to *istiḥsān* and the *qiyās* is held to be of no value, as if it did not exist at all. The *qiyās* in question is abandoned and discredited *ab initio* and it cannot therefore contradict *istiḥsān*, because a conflict can occur between two things of equal validity and strength, which is not the case here. Abū Zahrah has also confirmed that whenever one reads in the books of *fiqh* that analogy requires such and such and *istiḥsān* requires such and such, it does not mean that there are two equally valid positions. Rather there is only one valid ruling which is that of *istiḥsān*, unless it is a case in which some jurists have considered the ruling of *qiyās* to be stronger than that of *istiḥsān*. But even so, one of the two analogies will be seen as the obvious analogy and the other as the more subtle and effective analogy.[12] Al-Zarqā is also critical of al-Shāfiʿī, especially when al-Shāfiʿī equated *istiḥsān* with arbitrary law-making: 'In my view,' says al-Zarqā, 'it is an exaggeration on the part of Imam al-Shāfiʿī, because the *mujtahids* who resort to *istiḥsān* and *istiṣlāḥ* are only treading the path which the *Sharīʿah* has opened to them, as they are guided by indications provided in the text as well as the principles and objectives of *Sharīʿah*'.[13]

In conclusion, it may be said that *istiḥsān* became the focus of attention and provoked a vehement response from Imam al-Shāfiʿī and others partly because of the tendency that was generally observed of over-emphasis on *qiyās*. This is evident in Imam Shāfiʿī's methodology as he went on record to equate *qiyās* with *ijtihād* and to say that *qiyās* was *ijtihād* and *ijtihād* was *qiyās*. This was clearly an attempt on his part to narrow down the broader scope of *ijtihād* (and also of *ra'y*) to analogical reasoning alone. This was perhaps another instance where the Imam might have exaggerated the value of *qiyās*, possibly in order to curb extensive reliance on *ra'y* and unregulated *ijtihād*. Be that as it may, it remains to be said that part of the reason why *istiḥsān* became the focus of attention was because it was critical of *qiyās* and sought to regulate over-indulgence in it, and then offered a credible alternative to its rigidities. An over-emphasis on *qiyās*, in other words, accentuated the controversy over *istiḥsān*, which was in many ways seen as the antidote and regulator of *qiyās*.

If *istiḥsān* means acting on the stronger of two available indications, then acting on the weaker evidence must obviously be abandoned. But there is a difference of opinion on this. Al-Sarakhsī has addressed the question and refuted the view according to which one still has the choice of whether to act on *istiḥsān* or on the normal rule from which a departure has been suggested by that *istiḥsān*. Some latter-day jurists (*al-muta'akhkhirūn*) have held that acting on *istiḥsān* is preferable but acting on the normal rule or *qiyās* remains valid. Al-Sarakhsī considers this view imaginary and unreliable. For once a *qiyās* has been abandoned in favour of *istiḥsān*, then the ruling of that *qiyās* stands rejected and acting on it is no longer permissible. The theory of *istiḥsān* is clear on the point that it is stronger when it suggests a departure from an existing *qiyās*. The latter is therefore omitted and action may not be based on it, especially when there is direct conflict between the two rulings.

An example of *istiḥsān* that clashes with its related *qiyās* is the ruling of *istiḥsān* which holds the usurper (*ghāsib*) of landed property liable to compensation for the loss that occurs while the property is in his possession. This is the view of al-Shaybānī, one of the two disciples of Abū Ḥanīfa. Abū Ḥanīfa's other disciple, Abū Yūsuf, has held that the usurper is not liable for this loss according to normal rules (i.e. *qiyās*) but he is liable by way of *istiḥsān*. Thus when A usurps B's house and the house collapses, for unknown causes while in A's possession, the questions arise as to whether A should bear the loss for what he did not cause; whether A is liable at all; and whether his liability is confined to returning the property as it is, unless, of course, A has actually caused the collapse of the house in his possession. The majority of jurists have held the usurper liable for loss and damage of the property in his possession regardless of whether he might have caused it, whereas the minority view maintains otherwise. Since the two views are in conflict, it would be simply unfeasible to say that acting on either is permissible, and that one is the preferred view. *Istiḥsān* in this case means that the original ruling of *qiyās* is invalidated and abandoned.[14]

The same position is maintained in cases of textually-based *istiḥsān*. To say, for example, that lease and hire (*ijārah*), and advance payment sale (*salam*) have been validated by way of *istiḥsān*, notwithstanding the non-existence of the subject matter of both, means that they are valid contracts. Then to say that they are *ultra vires* under the rules of *qiyās* would mean invalidating something the *Sharīᶜah* has validated. The ruling of *qiyās* is therefore abandoned in favour of *istiḥsān*.

NOTES

1. Cf. al-Khudarī, *Tārīkh*, p. 201; Mūsā, Muḥammad Yūsuf. *Al-Madkhal li-Dirāsah al-Fiqh al-Islāmī*. 2nd. edn. Cairo: Dār al-Fikr al-ᶜArabī, 1373/1953, p. 198; Shaᶜbān, *Uṣūl*, p. 155; al-Zuḥaylī, Wahbah. *Uṣūl al-Fiqh al-Islāmī*. Damascus: Dār al-Fikr li'l-Ṭibāᶜah wa'l-Tawziᶜ wa'l-Nashr, 1406/1986, II, 740.

2. Al-Shāfiᶜi, Muḥammad b. Idris. *Kitāb al-Umm*. Cairo: Dār al-Shaᶜb, 1321AH, VII, 271-272.

3. Cf. Abū Zahrah, *Mālik*, par. 188, f.n.; Zarqā, *Al-Madkhal*, I, 115.

4. Al-Shāfiᶜī, *Al-Umm*, VI, 203; Al-Āmidī, *Iḥkām*, IV, 209; Mikādi, 'Baḥth fi'l-Istiḥsān', p. 317. The Companion, Khālid b. Walīd, who killed the person in that state had evidently applied his personal judgement, contrary to the normal rule that would exonerate from punishment anyone who recited the *kalimah shahādah* (testimonial of the faith). Khalid had acted as if by way of *istiḥsān*, because of the doubt over the genuineness of the profession. When the matter was brought to attention of the Prophet, he strongly disapproved the killing as arbitrary and indefensible.

5. Al-Āmidī, *Iḥkām*, IV, 210; Aḥmad Ḥasan, *Analogical Reasoning*, p. 411; Mikādi, 'al-Istiḥsān,' in *Usbuᶜ al-Fiqh*, p. 322.

6. Al-Sarakhsī, *Uṣūl*, II, 201; see also Kassim, 'Sarakhsī's Doctrine', p. 189; Mīqā, *Al-Ra'y*, p. 412.

7. Ibn Taymiya, *Mas'alah*, in Yūsuf, 'The Theory of *Istiḥsān*', p. 148.

8. Abū Zahrah, '*Taᶜlīq*', in *Usbuᶜ al-Fiqh*, pp. 362-363.

9. Ridwan Yūsuf, 'The Theory of *Istiḥsān*', p. 57.

10. Al-Naziᶜat, 79:40; Yūsuf, 12:53; al-Qasas, 28:50 respectively.

11. Al-Jīlānī, Abū'l-Qāsim b. Ḥasan. *Qawānīn al-Uṣūl*, Tehran: Dal al-Tababaᶜah ᶜAlī Qulikhan, 1299AH, p. 98; Mikādi, 'Baḥth fī'l Istiḥsān', p. 319.

12. Abū Zahrah, 'Taᶜlīq', in *Usbuᶜ al-Fiqh*, p. 363.

13. Zarqā, *Al-Madkhal*, I, 115.

14. Sarakhsī, *Uṣūl al-Sarakhsī*, II, 201ff.; al-Qurṭubī, Muḥammad b. Aḥmad b. Rushd. *Bidāyat al-Mujtahid wa Nihāyat al-Muqtasid*. Cairo: Muṣṭafā al-Bābī al-Ḥalabī, 1401/1981, II, 237.

CHAPTER SEVEN

Istiḥsān and Particularisation *(Takhṣīṣ)*

There are two aspects to this discussion, one of which addresses the question of whether *istiḥsān* is tantamount to specifying a general rule (*ḥukm*) of *Sharīᶜah*, or a ruling of *qiyās*, in connection with a certain issue. The other is an extension of the same point, but this time in reference to specifying the effective cause (*ᶜillah*) and through it the *ḥukm*, rather than specifying a *ḥukm* directly without particular reference to the *ᶜillah*. If one confirms the view that *istiḥsān* is in the nature of particularisation of the general, this implies that *istiḥsān* is not independent evidence. This is in fact in line with the Mālikī perspective on *istiḥsān* when it is said, for example, that *istiḥsān* consists of acting upon the stronger of two indications, or that it consists of acting on a particular benefit (*maṣlaḥah juz'iyyah*) vis-à-vis a general principle, by way of making an exceptional concession. This process resembles that of *takhṣīṣ al-ᶜumūm* or specifying a general text in order to uphold the spirit and purpose of that text. By resorting to *istiḥsān*, in other words, we are basically concerned with a better understanding of a general principle of *Sharīᶜah* and its proper implementation with reference to particular issues. Ibn al-ᶜArabī has seen *istiḥsān* in this light and has consequently observed that both Imam Mālik and Abū Ḥanīfah viewed *istiḥsān* as part of their understanding of specifying the general meaning of a text on any valid ground. Imam Mālik was more inclined to specify the general by reference to *maṣlaḥah* whereas Imam Abū Ḥanīfah would do so by reference to the saying of a Companion that was seen to be contrary to *qiyās*.[1] Both Imams Abū Ḥanīfah and Mālik saw *istiḥsān* as a specification of *qiyās* (*takhṣīṣ al-qiyās*) in the event where the application of *qiyās* in a particular instance departed from its own effective cause. While both Imams saw *istiḥsān* as a form of *takhṣīṣ*, the main difference between their respective approaches may be said to be that Imam Mālik took a broader view of both *takhṣīṣ* and *istiḥsān* by opening their scope to the requirements of *maṣlaḥah*, and he specified general texts by reference to *maṣlaḥah*; Imam Abū Ḥanīfah would on the other hand only take this course if it was upheld by a Companion. Al-Shāṭibī has explained the different approaches of the two Imams to *istiḥsān* as follows: in trying to understand the proper meaning of a general indication or evidence (*al-dalīl al-ᶜām*), Imam Mālik looked into the purpose and consequences of the law (*ma'ālāt al-aḥkām*), whereas Imam Abū Ḥanīfah's view of specification of the general text or *qiyās* was based on a specific text or saying of a Companion that warranted a departure from the general principle to a particular ruling.[2]

Ibn Taymiyyah (d. 728/1328) took a more flexible view of the particularisation of *ᶜillah*. He saw *istiḥsān* as a kind of particularisation of *ᶜillah* where the cause of the original *ḥukm*—which is being abandoned—is present but the *ḥukm* of that *ᶜillah* is absent due to an obstacle. In saying this Ibn Taymiyyah shared the view of the Muᶜtazilī scholar Abū'l-Ḥusayn al-Baṣrī (d. 436 AH) that the presence of an *ᶜillah* without its ruling *ḥukm* did not invalidate the *ᶜillah* and that the *ᶜillah* could exist without its relevant *ḥukm*. Both Ibn Taymiyyah and al-Baṣrī have held that the *ᶜillah* may be specified or even isolated from its *ḥukm* when the latter is obstructed. According to Ibn Taymiyyah, when the *ᶜillah* is rational and when the *mujtahid* can understand it, it may be either completely rejected, or modified to accommodate certain new cases which can be distinguished from the original case. It was in this way that Ibn Taymiyyah considered *istiḥsān* to be in the nature of *takhṣīṣ al-ᶜillah*, either through the modification of the *ᶜillah* or through its total nullification.

The opponents of *istiḥsān* have on the other hand asserted that *istiḥsān* violates one of the basic norms of rationality and law if it isolates the *ᶜillah* from its *ḥukm*, or makes an exception to the ruling *ḥukm* of a case despite the presence of its effective cause (*ᶜillah*). Stated simply, *takhṣīṣ al-ᶜillah* means the existence of a cause and the absence or suspension of its relevant ruling due to an obstacle. This implies that the advocates of *istiḥsān* can circumvent a *ḥukm*, say of the Qur'ān and *Sunnah*, by ignoring its effective cause. The critics of *istiḥsān* have said that in almost all the rulings of *istiḥsān*, there is an analogy which is rejected in favour of some text, consensus or a stronger analogy. The cause upon which the rejected analogy depends is still present in each case but without its expected legal effect. Without entering into details, it may briefly be stated that the Ḥanafīs have disagreed and replied that *istiḥsān* is not in the nature of *takhṣīṣ al-ᶜillah*; *istiḥsān* is a kind of *qiyās*. When we apply *istiḥsān*, the rule of law is established if the cause of that rule exists. In the event that the cause does not exist, the rule too does not exist.[3]

Ṣadr al-Sharīᶜah has categorically stated that *istiḥsān* is not in the nature of *takhṣīṣ al-ᶜillah*, despite the assertions of many to the contrary. This is because abandoning a *qiyās* for stronger evidence is not *takhṣīṣ al-ᶜillah*. The absence of a *ḥukm* in the case of *istiḥsān* is precisely due to the absence of an *ᶜillah*, and it is not a particularisation thereof. This is illustrated by reference to the oft-quoted example of the permissibility for human consumption of the leftovers of birds of prey, as opposed to the leftovers of predatory animals, which is prohibited simply because the *ᶜillah* of its prohibition, namely eating or drinking with the use of the tongue and the mixing therefore of saliva with the flesh of its catch, is present in the case of predators but is absent in the case of birds of prey. *Qiyās* in this case would extend the prohibition from the case of predator animals to birds of prey, but *istiḥsān* excludes the latter from the scope of that prohibition because of the absence of the effective cause. *Istiḥsān*, in other words, is not constructed on a mere specification of the *ᶜillah* of the *qiyās* in question, but derives its essence from the absence of, and total departure from, that *ᶜillah*.[4]

Al-Sarakhsī has strongly criticised those who validate the particularisation of *ᶜillah*. He admitted that there were some, even among the Ḥanafīs, who spoke approvingly of the idea of *takhṣīṣ al-ᶜillah* and held that it was valid. Sarakhsī attributed this tendency to the Muᶜtazilah and denied the basic validity of *takhṣīṣ al-ᶜillah*. In his *Uṣūl* he opened a chapter with the title, 'Explaining the corrupt view that validates *takhṣīṣ* of the Sharᶜī causes—*Faṣl fī Bayān Fasād al-Qawl bi-Jawāz al-Takhṣīṣ fī'l ᶜIlal al-Sharᶜiyyah*', and wrote that the approved position of our predecessors was that *takhṣīṣ al-ᶜillah* was impermissible and anyone who held otherwise 'was opposed to the followers of the *Sunnah* and affected by the *uṣūlī* views of the Muᶜtazilah'. Sarakhsī maintained that what is involved in the idea of *takhṣīṣ al-ᶜillah* amounted to logical contradiction (*al-tanāqud*) which is completely different from the basic idea of particularisation of the general (*al-takhṣīṣ*), to which there is no objection. Those who validate this logical incongruity, Sarakhsī adds, are saying in effect that a *ḥukm* of *Sharīᶜah* may be applied to some cases and may be suspended in other similar cases while the ᶜ*illah* is present in both cases, and what they say is for Sarakhsī totally corrupt and indefensible.[5]

NOTES

1. Cf. Al-Shāṭibī, *Muwāfaqāt*, IV, 208; Mīqā, *Al-Ra'y*, pp. 401 & 426.
2. Al-Shāṭibī, *Muwāfaqāt*, IV, 209; Mīqā, *Al-Ra'y*, p. 427.
3. Ibn Taymiyyah, *Mas'alah al-Istiḥsān*, in Makdisi, edr. *Arabic and Islamic Studies*, p. 458 ff; Ridwan Yūsuf, 'The Theory of *Istiḥsān*', pp. 65-67; Aḥmad Ḥasan, *Analogical Reasoning*, p. 422.
4. Ṣadr al-Sharīᶜah, *al-Tawdīh*, III, 10; *Mawsuᶜah*, IV, 46; Aḥmad Ḥasan, *Analogical Reasoning*, p. 422.
5. For further details see al-Sarakshī, *Uṣūl*, II, 208-210.

CHAPTER EIGHT

A Review of the Methodology of *Istiḥsān*

When the jurist is faced with a problem for which no direct ruling can be found in the text or *ijmāᶜ*, he may search for a precedent and try to find a solution by recourse to analogy. This he can do when his efforts lead him to the conclusion that the new issue falls under the rationale of existing law and shares the same effective cause with it. The early *ᶜulamā'* and *mujtahidūn* have generally identified analogy or *qiyās* as one of the principal instruments—indeed the main bastion—of *ijtihād*. *Qiyās* has been given a high profile in the methodology of *uṣūl al-fiqh* mainly because it is a guided form of *ijtihād* where the exercise of personal opinion *ra'y* is subservient to the textual guidance of the Qur'ān and *Sunnah*. In the event where *qiyās* is based on a ruling of general consensus or *ijmāᶜ*, its conformity with the basic guidance of revealed law is also assured. But since *qiyās* is founded on a particular effective cause, which is often identified by the *mujtahid*, it is possible that the *mujtahid* could fall into error, and this is why *qiyās* is classified as speculative (*ẓannī*) evidence.

The search for a pertinent analogy may reveal two different solutions, one of which is based on an obvious analogy and the other on a more subtle or hidden analogy. The latter is commonly equated with *istiḥsān*.

As explained earlier, there are basically two types of *istiḥsān*, namely analogical *istiḥsān* and exceptional *istiḥsān*. The former consists of a departure from obvious analogy (*qiyās jalī*) to a hidden analogy (*qiyās khafī*), whereas the latter consists of making an exception to the normal rules of *Sharīʿah* in particular cases. In both eventualities, the jurist relies on his personal opinion (*ra'y*) and carries out *ijtihād* on that basis for the purpose of avoiding the rigidity and hardship that are feared from strict conformity to existing law.

Both *qiyās* and *istiḥsān* must have an effective cause (*ʿillah*) and identification of the *ʿillah* in both cases is basically a rational exercise involving reliance on personal opinion and *ijtihād*. But in the case of analogy-based *istiḥsān* there is a two-fold recourse to *ʿillah*: one in the initial construction of *qiyās*, and the other in the abandonment of that *qiyās* for an alternative but preferable ruling. The jurist is thus more heavily involved in the exercise of *ra'y*, not only on account of the identification of the *ʿillah* on a two-tiered basis, but also in the decision to abandon the existing law for an alternative ruling. This is evidently a speculative exercise involving several *ra'y*-oriented steps and its accuracy and closeness to the obvious text can readily be open to question. The strength of *istiḥsān*, however, lies in the essence of that elaborate process and the conviction in which it must originate. The jurist is convinced that an alternative and a more appropriate solution must be found in order to serve the spirit and purpose of the law at the expense even of its letter, that is, if following the letter of the law frustrates the objectives of equity, *maṣlaḥah* and justice. This is partly why *istiḥsān*, consisting of a two-step analogy (*qiyās khafī*), is considered more effective and altogether preferable to obvious analogy (*qiyās jalī*). Having said this, one can also visualise the pitfalls of *istiḥsān* and the possibility that the jurist will exercise speculative judgement in his *ijtihād*. The two aspects of *istiḥsān*, representative at once of its inherent strength and weakness, have been manifested in the equally extreme positions that were taken by the two prominent Imams Abū Ḥanīfah and al-Shāfiʿī, one of whom advocated *istiḥsān* and the other rejected it altogether. Yet we note in the subsequent scholastic developments in almost all the leading schools of *fiqh* a general acknowledgement of the very positive yet sensitive role that *istiḥsān* can play in the adaptation of *Sharīʿah* to considerations of *maṣlaḥah* and social reality.

The need for a departure from the normal rules to an alternative ruling in *istiḥsān* is often justified in the name of necessity, benefit, removal of hardship, general consideration of equity and fairness (*iḥsān*) or indeed any combination of these. If there is a genuine case which has convinced the judge or the *mujtahid* of the need to make an exception, he will usually be able to find a particular basis for it by reference to one or a combination of these proofs. This aspect of the methodology of *istiḥsān* is very much like the rule that applies to adjudication and sentencing, namely that a judicial decision must explain its evidential basis and the reasons on which it is founded. There must, in other words, be an element of objectivity in the court decision which provides a visible basis for accountability, reassurance and review. The attempt on the part of the jurists of the Ḥanafī and Mālikī schools to elaborate the methodology of *istiḥsān* and expound the various bases on which it must be shown to have been based is basically sound as it stresses the objectivity and methodological accuracy in the construction of *istiḥsān*.

The theory of *istiḥsān* is evidently anchored in *qiyās* and derives much of its substance from *qiyās*. It may be noted, however, that recourse to *qiyās* or departure from one *qiyās* to another might have presented a useful method in the construction of *istiḥsān* at an early stage of the development of Islamic jurisprudence. This no longer seems to be the case after the passage of over a thousand years. It would appear that *qiyās* is not an interminable source and a great deal of its potential has probably already been exhausted. Text-based *qiyās* may consequently offer limited scope for the jurist and *mujtahid* in modern times. Since a *sharᶜī qiyās* can only be constructed on the basis of an existing *ḥukm* in the higher sources, and since the clear injunctions of the text and *ijmāᶜ* are limited in number, *qiyās* may no longer be expected to provide a particularly rich and dynamic base for *istiḥsān*.

There are also limitations on the exercise of *qiyās* in judicial decision-making. This is partly due to the fact that judicial precedent, which is a recognised source of law in the common law system, is not a recognised source under the *uṣūl al-fiqh*. Judicial precedent is to a large extent an embodiment of analogical reasoning and the application of the ruling of higher courts to new but similar cases that are brought before the lower courts. A rich legacy of case law that has been developed in the common law jurisdiction is largely due to the binding force that common law has recognised for judicial precedent. Without wishing to enter into detail, the facts are that the structure and methodology of *qiyās* that we have in Islamic jurisprudence have become somewhat over-burdened by technicality. This situation is also not helped by the fact that juridical precedent is not a recognised source in *uṣūl al-fiqh*. If there are limitations on the resourcefulness and utility of *qiyās*, one can imagine that the situation is not likely to be any better for analogy-based *istiḥsān*,which consists of not one, but two analogies. One may also note here the point referred to earlier about the inherent difficulty involved in the exercise of this two-tiered *qiyās*, which is the proposed basis of Ḥanafī *istiḥsān*. Supposing that a jurist can think of an alternative analogy to the one that is known as obvious analogy, it must at times be difficult to identify which is the more effective of the two, the obvious *qiyās* or the hidden *qiyās*. Even the distinction as to which may be said to be the obvious analogy, as opposed to the hidden, can be decidedly speculative and complex. One can imagine that if *qiyās* itself is not effectively utilised, partly because of the elaborate series of conditions that are attached to each of the four pillars thereof, especially the *ᶜillah*, then how much more can one say about a two-tiered *qiyās* or *istiḥsān*, which involves identification of another *ᶜillah* in addition to the one that underlay the first *qiyās*. Analogical *istiḥsān* may therefore be attempted in some cases but it would appear to have its limitations.

One way to reduce technicality in this procedure might be to ignore the distinction between *qiyās jalī* and *qiyās khafī* but to retain the analogical basis of the formula that is involved. This might mean that the new *qiyās* proposed in relation to a particular case, which is designed to offer a preferable alternative, may just be considered a preferable *qiyās* or *qiyās mustaḥsan*, as it has in fact been called, regardless of how it might relate to the original *qiyās* that is supposed to have been abandoned. This would open up the methodology of analogy-based *istiḥsān* by doing away with the distinction between *qiyās jalī* and *qiyās khafī* and retaining instead a simpler variety of analogical *istiḥsān* which consists of a preferable *qiyās*.

As for the *istiḥsān* which consists of making an exception to existing law, one may draw attention to two or three points on this score. One of these has already been discussed in the works of *ᶜulamā'* like al-Ghazālī, al-Āmidī and others, to the effect that when departure from an existing rule is justified on the authority of higher proofs such as the Qur'ān, *Sunnah* and *ijmāᶜ*, the exception made is not *istiḥsān* in its technical sense but a normative ruling of the Qur'ān, *Sunnah* or *ijmāᶜ*, as the case may be.

Secondly, in view of what has just been stated, a certain adjustment to the conventional typology of *istiḥsān* might be advisable: at the one end of the spectrum, we have the textually-based *istiḥsān* founded on the authority of the Qur'ān and *Sunnah*, which we now propose to exclude from the typology of *istiḥsān*. It has been explained elsewhere that the authority of the Qur'ān and *Sunnah* is normative and stands above the level of *istiḥsān*. The *mujtahid* may, of course, seek support for his efforts in the authority of the higher proofs. What is proposed here is merely to change the format and typology of *istiḥsān*. Then at the other end of the spectrum, one might propose to add, as explained earlier, two other types of *istiḥsān* that are founded on considerations of equity (*iḥsān*) and removal of hardship (*rafᶜ al-ḥaraj*). The substance of this proposal is not new as both originate in the Qur'ān and the *ᶜulamā'* have often acted on them in their juristic endeavours. The suggested adjustment is therefore one of format, which seeks a clearer identification of the evidential bases of *istiḥsān*. One can, in fact, find instances of recourse to *istiḥsān* inspired by considerations of equity and *rafᶜ al-ḥaraj* in the precedent of the Companions, especially that of the Caliph ᶜUmar ibn al-Khaṭṭāb, in the case of inheritance known as al-Mushtarakah, which we discussed above.

Thirdly, in evaluating the evidential basis of *istiḥsān*, one could consider taking an approach combining those of the Ḥanafīs and Mālikīs. If we take the Mālikī approach to the underlying evidence of *istiḥsān*, then consideration is given in the first place to the stronger of two proofs or indications. This is probably when the *mujtahid* sees the general picture and reaches a state of mind which leaves him in no doubt about the need for an alternative solution to the problem, and he knows which of the two conceivable solutions is preferable. The next step is to specify the nature of the two indications and articulate the type of *istiḥsān* that is being attempted. The *mujtahid*, in other words, needs to specify whether the departure from one solution to another is supported by considerations of *maṣlaḥah*, removal of hardship, necessity or *ᶜurf*. At this stage the *mujtahid* will have acted on the Ḥanafī approach of identifying the specific basis of *istiḥsān* in the interests of objectivity and methodological transparence.

With reference to the effective cause (*ᶜillah*) of *istiḥsān*, there is no question that analogy-based *istiḥsān* must proceed upon an identifiable *ᶜillah*. For *qiyās*, whether initial or secondary, cannot be constructed without an *ᶜillah*, and this is precisely the position with regard to analogical *istiḥsān*. But we can perhaps say this generally about all varieties of *istiḥsān*, that abandoning a rule of law, or a *qiyās*, for a better alternative is always for a certain reason. One can hardly imagine that such a deliberate move could be without a cause. One would normally expect the basic rationale and motivation of the whole exercise to be unmistakably clear, and in any case strong enough to warrant abandonment of existing rules in connection with particular issues. Only in cases where the departure in question finds clear support in the textual evidence of the higher proofs, especially the Qur'ān and *Sunnah*, would it be a matter of applying the latter, and the exercise is then likely to fall within the ambit of interpretation and understanding of the text which may not require an elaborate search for the *ʿillah*. Even so, it is proposed, for the sake mainly of clarity and the avoidance of personal preference, that the basic cause and rationale of *istiḥsān*, whether analogical or exceptional, should normally be identified in any attempt at constructing *istiḥsān*. In doing so, it should be sufficient to identify either the specific *ʿillah* in its technical sense, as in the case of conventional *qiyās*,[1] or the benefit and purpose of the proposed *istiḥsān*, and the mischief or harm that it seeks to prevent. One would imagine that the basic structure of *istiḥsān* in almost all its varieties is such that reference to these is almost inevitable, and if there is a good case, it should not be difficult to identify the cause and underlying rationale of the proposed change through the modality of *istiḥsān*. If there is more than one *ʿillah* consisting of a variety of influences, one may identify more than one, and I do not propose a highly technical approach to the identification of the *ʿillah*.

To identify an *ʿillah* for every instance of departure from the normal rules by way of *istiḥsān* would also have the effect of making *istiḥsān* transferable to similar cases when the *ʿillah* for it applies. For otherwise *istiḥsān* is for the most part concerned with making exceptions, and the law of exception is not transferable as it is expected to be confined to the exceptional case to which it is linked. But then when the *ʿillah* of a departure, or exception, to existing law is clearly articulated, there basically remains no reason why a similar departure cannot be attempted in other similar cases. In this sense, exception-based *istiḥsān* stands on a similar footing to *qiyās*, which means that both are transferable to similar cases, as both operate on the basis of an effective cause.

The remaining part of this volume identifies and discusses some issues of economic interest where *istiḥsān* can be utilised in the search for alternative solutions to some issues of contemporary interest.

NOTES

1. A discussion of the *ʿillah*, in conjunction with *qiyās*, can be found in Kamali, *Jurisprudence*, p. 274ff.

PART TWO

CONTEMPORARY APPLICATIONS

Introduction

Part Two of this volume addresses a number of issues pertaining to the Islamic law of sale and partnership as well as issues that have arisen in the area of charitable endowments (*awqāf*). The main purpose of this enquiry is to identify the issues and suggest preferable or alternative solutions for them through the application of *istiḥsān*. A certain number of issues have been identified in relation to the contract of sale and its requirement in particular of taking into possession (*qabḍ*) the subject matter of sale, matters pertaining to Islamic banking in the areas especially of commenda (*muḍārabah*), partnership (*mushārakah*), and profit added sale (*murābaḥah*). I have looked into the applied aspects of these modes of transaction as they are currently practiced by Islamic banks in the context of trade financing and investment. The main issue of concern here is that partnership financing in the forms of *muḍārabah* and *mushārakah*, although of central importance to the basic philosophy and goals of Islamic banking, has been on the decline and has never played a significant role in the overall operations of Islamic banks.

These issues are broad and in all likelihood would need to be addressed from various angles by experts in other related disciplines. My own enquiry into them is basically confined to exploring the potential of *istiḥsān* in the search for better alternatives. The issues are not new as many scholars and commentators have addressed them and spoken at length about them within and outside the purview of Islamic jurisprudence, yet hardly any attempt seems to have been made to look into these issues from the perspective of *istiḥsān*. The conclusions I have drawn and the suggestions I make are generally tentative and may well be open to further enquiry and research. By its very essence, *istiḥsān* involves a quest for better and preferable alternatives; the researcher is inevitably engaged in a process which necessitates recourse to juristic speculation and *ra'y*. Although the effort that this exercise involves is always to be guided by valid *sharʿī* evidence, the choice of a particular method and the manner in which it is formulated and presented here may well be in need of further refinement, and I therefore welcome readers' comments and contributions towards further improvements that might be based on a more penetrating analysis of the issues involved.

CHAPTER NINE

The Issue of *Qabḍ* (taking possession)

The requirement that sales and purchases of commodities, especially foodstuffs, must be preceded and succeeded by actual possession of the goods involved is laid down in the ḥadīth, as discussed below, and has received considerable attention in the scholastic works of the ʿulamā' on the subject. These scholastic approaches towards *qabḍ* tend to vary from one school to another and there is much diversity of opinion about the meaning of *qabḍ* and the manner in which it takes place in relation to different types of goods, whether movable or immovable, and the category in which they fall, such as foodstuffs as opposed to other commodities, and even the manner in which they were acquired in the first place, whether through purchase, gift or inheritance, as well as the relevance of all this to prevailing custom and the realities of the market-place. I begin this discussion with a perusal of the ḥadīth, followed by an overview of the *fiqh* positions on *qabḍ*, and lastly turn to whether *istiḥsān* can be invoked in order to relax the requirement of *qabḍ* in relation, for example, to guaranteed delivery sales and also the proposed scripless trading of stocks and shares in the stock market.

The basic requirement of *qabḍ* has been laid down in a ḥadīth narrated by ʿAbd Allāh ibn ʿUmar from the Blessed Prophet:

> 'He who buys foodstuffs should not sell them till he has received them.'[1]

من ابتاع طعاما فلا يبعه حتى يقبضه

In another ḥadīth, also reported by ʿAbd Allāh ibn ʿUmar, the Blessed Prophet said:

> 'He who buys foodstuffs should not sell them until he is satisfied with the measure with which he has bought them.'[2]

من ابتاع طعاما فلا يبعه حتى يستوفيه

In yet a third report on the same subject Ibn ʿAbbās narrated the following ḥadīth from the Blessed Prophet:

> 'He who buys foodstuffs should not sell them until he has taken possession of them. Ibn ʿAbbās said: "I think this applies to all other things as well".'[3]

من ابتاع طعاما فلا يبعه حتى يستوفيه.
قال ابن عباس واحسب كل شيء مثله

Despite the fact that some prominent ʿulamā', including Imam al-Shāfiʿī, have followed Ibn ʿAbbās's version of the above ḥadīth in their *fatwā* and have consequently laid down that *qabḍ* is a requirement not only for foodstuffs but all other things also, the actual text of the ḥadīth is concerned with foodstuffs only. Ibn ʿAbbās's generalisation is evidently in the nature of an analogy, which is possibly less warranted and decidedly speculative: had it been the intention of the ḥadīth to convey a general ruling, it would have provided some indication to that effect, which is not the case.

The basic purpose of *qabḍ* is to ensure that the seller is able to make delivery of what he sells, and the concern here is mainly with foodstuffs which may be perishable and liable to destruction and loss. To ensure delivery, the ḥadīth requires that foodstuffs must be taken into possession prior to resale. For if the buyer sells the foodstuffs he has purchased before taking them into possession, he will have indulged in risk-taking and uncertainty (*gharar*) in relation to the prospects of delivery. It is stated in the *Hidāyah* that the Prophet prohibited the sale of commodities, especially perishable ones, which the seller did not possess, because of uncertainty about their delivery to the buyer.[4]

The question that now arises is whether strict conformity to the ruling of the ḥadīth, in certain areas of sale, serves its original purpose or not and whether or not it is to be attended by its effective cause (*ᶜillah*), which is to prevent *gharar*. If there is an area of sale where delivery is guaranteed in a way that precludes even the slightest uncertainty, then surely insisting on the requirement of *qabḍ* will not have the same meaning and may well amount to a mechanical application of the text in situations where its proper *ᶜillah* is no longer present. If there is such a case then one ought to be able to make a suitable exception, by recourse to *istiḥsān*, to the existing rules of *qabḍ*, and make the law consistent with the reality of the market-place. In some cases, as I shall elaborate, customary practice and market reality has followed a course that has already adopted the necessary changes even ahead of any change in the relevant rules of *fiqh*. In that situation one might be inclined to think that social reality and custom have made the rules either totally or partially redundant, and the only advisable course for the jurist to take might be to acknowledge the change by making the necessary exception to the normal rule, especially when this can find support either in specific evidence or the general spirit and objectives of the Sharīᶜah.

One may not need to insist on actual possession by the seller of the commodity in question if delivery is, for example, guaranteed by reliable individuals or institutions or when delivery is assured by indisputable documents such as warehouse warrants, or guarantees by a bank or a clearing-house. In circumstances such as these, the seller may, on grounds of *istiḥsān* based on *maṣlaḥah* (and *ᶜurf*), be exempted from the requirements of taking possession prior to resale. The effective cause of this concession may be said to be the absence of doubt and uncertainty (*gharar*) about the prospects of delivery, especially when the sale involves a standard delivery procedure that inspires total confidence of the seller's ability to fulfil his contractual obligations. The benefit of this would be to facilitate the easy flow of market transactions, especially in the area of the bulk trade of commodities, where the terms of the trade establish a certain procedure that makes the questions of weighing, measuring and *qabḍ* almost unnecessary and even cumbersome.

The question of *qabḍ* also arises with regard to the scripless sale of stocks and shares, which is an emerging trend that has already been adopted in some countries, including Malaysia. The Kuala Lumpur Stock Exchange carried out its plan to phase out, by the end of 1996, the physical exchange of share certificates and made preparations started in 1993, to shift over to scripless trading. A new central depositing system is now in place where all prospective traders and customers are required to formally register with this organisation. The details of the registration procedure are such that they guarantee the reliability and to some extent the credit-worthiness of the registered traders. Only after the due completion of registration formalities will the customer be able to trade in stocks and shares. Scripless trading is planned with the purpose particularly of eliminating the need for the physical transfer and delivery of share certificates, which has proven to be time-consuming and cumbersome. Preparations were made in Malaysia for the sales and purchases of stocks to become entirely computerised, and it is now a matter of crediting and debiting customer accounts without involving the physical delivery or taking into possession of share certificates. The shift to the new system was to take place in stages and about eight hundred listed stocks on the Kuala Lumpur Stock Exchange completed the required preparations, and the shift to scripless trading of stocks and shares was completed according to plan. It seems that there will still be share certificates issued by the companies and also deposited with the stock exchange but without any name or number. Only when a customer wishes to cease trading and withdraws from the market completely can share certificates be issued in his name. But for current trading, there is no physical delivery and exchange of share certificates. Another advantage of the new system is with reference to safe-keeping. Previously, share certificates were often lost or stolen and were occasionally the subject of forgery and false reporting, and all of this was to be remedied through scripless trading. Here we had, I believe, a case for a *maṣlaḥah*-based *istiḥsān* which meant a departure from existing law concerning *qabḍ* to an alternative ruling on an exceptional basis. The normal rules of *qabḍ* will naturally remain applicable and will continue to govern the conventional contract of sale and sale transactions in the open market where delivery is, broadly speaking, not guaranteed. The stock market represents an exception in that it is a highly centralised and controlled market where effective regulatory measures can be taken and changes introduced and implemented, at short notice, whenever necessary, and also discontinued and withdrawn in the event where existing regulations run into obstacles.

A certain measure of support for our analysis can also be found in the works of the Ḥanbalī scholars Ibn Taymiyyah, his disciple Ibn Qayyim, and Ibn Qudāmah whose views on the subject of *qabḍ* marked a departure from the majority position. By opening up the concept of *qabḍ* to the influence of custom, the Ḥanbalī ʿulamā' have injected a degree of dynamism into *qabḍ* which makes the whole concept essentially adaptable to different situations. Ibn Taymiyyah criticised the literalist orientation of the majority opinion, which confined the meaning of *qabḍ* to holding and retention (*ḥabs*) or evacuation (*takhliyah*) and the like, and stated that no specific meaning had been given to *qabḍ* either in the Arabic language or in Sharīʿah. *Qabḍ* in the sense of evacuation for instance varied from object to object and the manner in which evacuation occurs is not always the same. The precise meaning of *qabḍ* is therefore to be determined by reference to prevailing custom.[5]

Ibn Qudāmah has also stated that *qabḍ* in all things refers to an appropriate manner of taking possession. The Sharīʿah has stipulated *qabḍ* but the manner in which it is to be accomplished is determined by custom. It may consist of holding and retention, taking into custody (*al-ḥirz*), evacuation (*takhliyah*), separating (*al-tafarruq*) and even viewing (*al-mushāhadah*). *Qabḍ* is required for all fungible commodities that are sold by weight, measurement and number. This is so partly because the responsibility for destruction and loss (*al-ḍamān*) in such commodities is transferred to the buyer after *qabḍ*, and *qabḍ* in respect of such goods takes place when they are weighed and measured. As for goods which are not sold by measurement and weight, such as clothes and livestock, they may be sold even prior to *qabḍ*. The reason for this is that liability for the destruction and loss of such items devolves upon the buyer prior to *qabḍ*, that is, at the time of the conclusion of contract.[6]

Qabḍ in the sale of food grains that are sold by measurement and weight takes place upon measurement (note that wheat and barley were sold by measurement during the Prophet's lifetime; their sale by weight is a recent practice). When food grains are bought in lump sum (*juzāfan*), they are taken into possession, according to Imam Shāfiʿī, when they are physically removed. The requirement of *qabḍ* is on the other hand omitted, in the sale of both foodstuffs and real property, in the event where ownership is transferred by ways other than purchase, such as through gift and inheritance. In such cases they may also be sold prior to *qabḍ*, because gifts and inheritance involve no financial exchange, and the seller is not committed to the payment of a price to someone else.[7]

It is interesting to note that Ibn Ḥazm al-Ẓāhirī has confined the application of the ḥadiths on *qabḍ* to one item only, namely wheat. He concluded that the sale of everything is lawful prior to taking possession except for wheat. The reason for this interpretation, according to Ibn Ḥazm, is that the word '*taʿām*' which occurs in the ḥadīth means wheat and nothing else, because *taᶜām* during the lifetime of the Prophet was being used in this sense alone.

The Ḥanbalī ᶜulamā' have thus understood *qabḍ* to be a relatively open concept which is amenable to the changing influences of commercial reality and custom. With the exception perhaps of the Shāfiᶜīs, none of the other schools require *qabḍ* prior to sale in immovable objects. The Mālikīs have confined *qabḍ* to foodgrains only. *Qabḍ* in fungible goods takes place, as noted above, when they are measured for the purpose of delivery. In at least two varieties of sale, namely the advance payment sale of *salam* and the manufacturing contract (*istiṣnāᶜ*), the requirement of *qabḍ* has been omitted altogether, and the exemption here extends to all goods including food grains. *Salam* and *istiṣnāᶜ* were validated on grounds of utility and convenience.

In the bulk sale of food grains, large quantities are nowadays bought and sold in standardised quantities and packages that are weighed, sealed and labelled accordingly, so that there remains no need to weigh them each time they are sold. Sometimes warehouse documents provide evidence of the quantities involved, and it would appear that *qabḍ* in such commodities takes place in subsequent transactions, following the initial packaging, through the examination and transfer of relevant documents, rather than weighing and measuring again and again.

Customary practice thus plays an important role in determining the manner in which the legal requirements of delivery and *qabḍ* may be fulfilled. Provided that the process adopted for these purposes is free of uncertainty (*gharar*) and the likelihood of giving rise to disputes, it may be acceptable even if it transforms the initial concept of physical retention into an altogether different procedure. In banking transactions, the record of accounts (*al-qayḍ al-ḥisābī*) is generally accepted in both Islamic and conventional banks as the equivalent of actual *qabḍ* (*al-qabḍ al-haqīqī*).[8] It is quite conceivable that modern technology and computerisation may bring further changes into the conventional concept of *qabḍ*, and these may gain popularity and customary approval. This process would be acceptable from the viewpoint of the Sharīᶜah if it fulfils the basic rationale of *qabḍ*, which is to prevent uncertainty and *gharar* concerning the seller's ability to deliver.

The above analysis proposes a certain departure, by way of exceptional *istiḥsān*, from the ruling of ḥadīth on *qabḍ*, and the *istiḥsān* that is so proposed is based on prevailing reality and custom. The effective cause (*ᶜillah*) of this *istiḥsān* may be said to be, in addition to the one suggested above (i.e. the absence of *gharar*), to facilitate ease and convenience for the people. But the departure is proposed only in some cases, namely the bulk sale of fungible commodities where customary practice and established procedures make *qabḍ* prior to resale either unnecessary or inconvenient. I have also made out a case for customary practice regarding *qabḍ* where records of accounts and documentary evidence may be seen as acceptable substitutes to the conventional idea of *qabḍ* in the sense of physical transfer and the retention of objects. These departures are in the nature of exceptional *istiḥsān*, and proceed on the assumption that the normal rules of *qabḍ* will remain applicable to all other cases outside scope of the proposed exceptions.

NOTES

1. Al-Bukhārī, III, p. 194.
2. Ibid, III, p. 191.
3. Ibid., III, p. 195.
4 Al-Marghinānī, the *Hidāya* (Hamilton's trans.), p. 275.
5. Ibn Taymiyyah, *Majmūᶜah Fatāwā*, X, 375.
6. Ibn Qudāmah, *Al-Mughnī*, IV, 124 ff.
7. Al-Shāfiᶜī, *Al-Umm*, III, 60; al-Jundī, *Muᶜāmalāt*, p. 122.
8. Cf. Sāmī Ḥamoud, *Taṭwīr al-Aᶜmal al-Maṣrafiyyah bi-ma Yattafiq wa al-Sharīᶜah al-Islāmiyyah*, 2nd edn. Oman: Maṭbaᶜah al-Sharq, 1402/1982, p. 346ff.

CHAPTER TEN

Issues Pertaining to *Awqāf* (charitable endowments)

Several questions have been raised concerning *waqf* properties and their economic viability under the present circumstances both within Muslim countries and in minority Muslim communities. Thus according to one observer 'the present circumstances in Muslim countries are not conducive to the institution of *waqf*. This vital Islamic institution designed to serve important social and economic purposes is facing the danger of total annihilation.'[1] Some of the causes of this decline include inefficient bureaucratic control of *waqf* by government institutions. The control of *waqf* by government has apparently marked a total departure from the *fiqhī* regime which designated *waqf* a privately managed institution. Under *fiqh* rules, the courts of justice should have only limited powers to intervene in the event of manifest abuse and in the interests of the safety and protection of *waqf* property. Yet there arose much dissatisfaction with the inefficiency and abuse displayed by incompetent administrators, which meant that a certain measure of government intervention was necessary in order to prevent the mismanagement and deterioration of *waqf* properties. But instead of achieving a reasonable combination between the two influences, what we have is total bureaucratic control which is also inefficient and suffers from all the familiar flaws of public enterprises, such as lack of incentive and misuse of authority. This situation has reached a critical stage whereby 'private *awqāf* are becoming extinct,'[2] and people are not encouraged to establish them any more. Land Reform legislation in many countries has also imposed limits on land holding and this has in turn encouraged a splitting up of agricultural estates among family members, which in the final analysis works as a disincentive to the setting up of *awqāf*. We may note here that private *awqāf* do not fall under government jurisdiction, yet they too face the danger of extinction. The main reason for this is the fixation of ceilings on agricultural holdings under the land reform laws introduced in many countries including Egypt, Syria, Turkey, Bangladesh and Pakistan. Land owners are thus tempted to divide large agricultural estates among family members, each getting the share permissible under land reform regulations.[3]

Al-Zarqā has highlighted the problem of the low liquidity of *awqāf*, as they are usually in real estates and the assets involved cannot be easily transferred to more profitable projects. The question is then raised as to whether it is permissible to invest the assets of *waqf* in other areas by buying, for example, shares in a company that is engaged in lawful activities. Another question raised is whether it is permissible, especially in the case of small landholdings, to sell a number of *awqāf* in real estates that exist in one city or district and invest the proceeds in a single but profitable project in the same locality or elsewhere in the same country.[4] And lastly the question has arisen as to the position of *waqf* in minority Muslim communities. One aspect of the discussion here refers to a situation where a deceased Muslim who resided in a non-Muslim community left no legal heirs to inherit his property. Under the present legal framework, this property goes to the secular government's exchequer. 'Was there a provision', the question was asked 'in the Sharīᶜah to transfer such a property to the *awqāf*?' Then it was added that this particular property should go to general charities and not to the *awqāf* 'because for *awqāf* the will of the dedicator must be known and obtained.'[5]

Another question raised in this context is that of whether *awqāf* can collaborate with the programmes of such other international bodies and institutions as FAO, UNICEF and WHO. And if this is not feasible for certain reasons, one might ask whether the IDB could provide technical assistance to *awqāf* institutions in co-operation with these international agencies. It is believed that Sharīᶜah-based answers to these questions 'will greatly affect the operation of *awqāf* institutions in the Muslim minority regions.'[6]

There are evidently many questions which require deep inquiry into the *fiqhī* regulations pertaining to ownership, inalienability and the permanence of the *awqāf* and so on. Delving deep into these issues would, however, be beyond the scope of the present research—and some of these issues may best be approached, perhaps, through other avenues than *istiḥsān*, but it seems that *istiḥsān* does relate to some of them. The responses I have attempted below to some of the *waqf*-related issues are within this framework, and are generally tentative.

To begin with one should note that the rules of *fiqh* pertaining to *waqf* are almost entirely the product of juristic *ijtihād* as there are no specific injunctions in the Qur'ān or Sunnah on the subject. The supportive evidence for *waqf* that is found in the Qur'ān is in the nature of general exhortation and encouragement in numerous places, of charity and the giving of generous help to those in need, and acts that would fall under the broad concept of the promotion of benevolent and good works (Cf. Āl-ᶜImrān, 3:92; al-Baqarah, 2:110). The Qur'ān is emphatic on this and the Sunnah not only endorses the Qur'ān, but *waqf* finds its original precedent in the Sunnah of the Prophet.[7] Yet the detailed *fiqh* regulations pertaining to the various aspects of *waqf* were formulated in line with the prevailing conditions of the time when the need for such rules was felt in view of the ever-increasing size and significance of *waqf* properties. It is therefore proposed that one should follow the rules of *fiqh* in so far as they remain beneficial, relevant and conducive to the continuity and well-being of this important institution. Some of these rules, such as those pertaining to respect for private property, are not merely based in speculative *ijtihād* but have decisive support in the higher proofs. But if there is convincing evidence to indicate that some of the *ijtihādī* rules of *fiqh*, which were evidently suitable within their respective time frames, no longer offer a suitable response to the current problems of the Muslim community and *ummah*, then those rules may be changed and replaced, and total inertia in the face of possible prejudice and harm would be against the normative teachings of the Qur'ān and Sunnah.

The basic Sharīᶜah guidance here is that harm must be eliminated (*al-ḍararu yuzāl*) as we read in a legal maxim of *fiqh*, which is in fact merely a re-stating of the ḥadīth that 'harm shall neither be tolerated nor reciprocated.' It is also provided in another legal maxim that 'harm is to be prevented to the extent that is possible.'[8] The guidance here is general in that it requires affirmative action in the face of prejudice and harm. Since no particular methods are specified for the elimination of harm, nor can it be expected that such measures could all be specified in advance, any means that are effective and relevant and do not conflict with the rest of the Sharīᶜah may be adopted. The substance of this guidance is, of course, not specific to *istiḥsān*, yet a ruling of *istiḥsān* may well be formulated in pursuit of its objective and purpose.

Awqāf are permanent and irrevocable, which means that once a legally competent person assigns his property into *waqf*, the dedicator (*wāqif*) relinquishes his proprietary rights and cannot revoke the *waqf*. It may either be a public or a private *waqf*. In the case of a public *waqf*, the dedication of property is exclusively for public purposes such as building and upkeep of mosques, *madrasahs*, hospitals and the like. The beneficiaries of a private *waqf*, or family endowment, are on the other hand one's family and relatives. A private *waqf* of long-standing whose beneficiaries have passed away or are no longer known may eventually evolve into a public *waqf*. The *wāqif* may specify his intentions as to the purpose of *waqf*, the manner of its utilisation and its devolution among the beneficiaries. The purpose is always charitable, humanitarian, and pious and must pursue lawful objectives.

The first administrator (*mutawallī*) of *waqf* is usually appointed by the *wāqif*, and the judge (*qādī*) has the right of supervision over the *waqf* to prevent manifest mismanagement and abuse. The history of *awqāf* indicates that the courts have also intervened in instances of questionable dedications when *waqf* has been used as a means of defeating the rights of creditors or as a means of interference with the rules of inheritance. Notwithstanding the key role that the *mutawallī* plays in the management of *waqf*, his administrative powers are nevertheless limited to the extent stipulated in the instrument of *waqf*, or the court order which may be issued in the best interest of *waqf*. In the event, for example, when the *mutawallī* has not been authorised by the *wāqif* to sell or mortgage the *waqf* property, and this is later considered to be in the best interest of *waqf*, a court order must be obtained to authorise the sale or mortgage of the *waqf* property. In the event where neither the *wāqif* nor the *mutawallī* have made a provision as to who should succeed the *mutawallī*, the court has the power to appoint a *mutawallī*. The court is also authorised to replace the *mutawalli* when he refuses to discharge his duties or becomes imcapacitated and no longer capable of office.

The majority ruling of the leading *madhāhib*, excepting Imam Abu Ḥanīfah, is that *waqf* is irrevocable and once the dedication is properly made neither the *wāqif*, nor the beneficiary, nor even the judge, has the authority to revoke it. Imam Abu Ḥanīfah has on the other hand held that the *wāqif* retains the right of ownership and is entitled to revoke the *waqf*. This is because he identifies *waqf* as belonging to the category of non-binding contracts (*ᶜaqd jā'iz*) such as a temporary loan (*ᶜāriyah*) which does not bind its owner and he may therefore revoke it.[9] So here we have two different positions in the established rules of *fiqh* which may offer a basis on which to construct *istiḥsān*. If one considers the irrevocability of *waqf* to be the normal position, Imam Abu Ḥanīfah's opinion may be adopted as a preferable alternative in exceptional situations where revocability may seem to be the best solution to the dilemma of a rapidly dilapidating *waqf* property. In order to ensure reliability and confidence in the operation of this *istiḥsān*, the decision to declare a particular *waqf* revocable should be issued by a competent judge, preferably a Sharīᶜah judge, wherever possible. In the absence of a Sharīᶜah judge, the civil court in the locality should be authorised to declare a particular *waqf* revocable. In either case the decision should be based on documentary evidence that might comprise a full enquiry and report on the *waqf* property concerned. A committee for that purpose may be appointed by the court, which may include the *waqf* administrator (*mutawallī*) and two other suitably qualified individuals to prepare a report and make recommendations to the court.

The effective cause (*ᶜillah*) of declaring a *waqf* revocable should be to prevent damage, deterioration and loss to the *waqf* property and the purpose would naturally be to turn a loss-making situation into a financially viable and profitable proposition. In declaring the *waqf* revocable, the judge should act out of conviction which is more than just a balance of probabilities, and the alternative that is contemplated should be preferable by reference to the valid evidence of Sharīᶜah and its overriding objectives.

When it is proposed that *waqf* may be declared revocable, the suggestion is made within the given *fiqhī* framework of *waqf* and its basic postulate that *waqf* is a permanent dedication of valuable property. In the event of declaring a particular *waqf* revocable, the purpose is to maintain the permanence of that *waqf* in that the assets that are dedicated to a charitable cause should remain dedicated to the same purpose, except a change of direction in the way it is utilised is felt necessary and the only way to achieve this is to terminate the original *waqf* and institute a new one as a substitute. This may involve the sale of the property of *waqf* for the purpose of liquidity in order to facilitate the setting up of a more profitable *waqf* with the same objective as the one it is proposed to replace. The judge who revokes the *waqf* and declares it terminated may in the meantime appoint a committee to supervise the sale and re-investment of the assets of *waqf* and report back to the court with the results, which will become binding with the ratification and approval of the court. The supervisory committee should normally include, and possibly be headed by, the *mutawallī* of the *waqf* in question, whose co-operation and counsel should be solicited and considered. Only in circumstances where the *mutawallī* himself is deemed to have been responsible, wholly or in part, for the deterioration of the *waqf* property may the court act independently, and it may decide not to include him in the supervisory committee. In that eventuality and in all cases of serious neglect of duty and mismanagement, the court may also consider appointing another *mutawallī* and place him in charge of the new *waqf*.

The committee which reports and makes recommendations to the court that a *waqf* should be declared revocable should also be asked to give an opinion as to the best alternative method of investment for the revenues of *waqf* once these are realised. If it seems advisable that two, three or several *awqāf* in the locality should all be pooled together in one financially viable project, the court in the locality may consider this and make appropriate decisions. This may involve revocation of several *awqāf* in the locality in order to set up a new *waqf* on a partnership basis, each entering a fiduciary relationship with the other for common objectives. The terms of this merger and the necessary stipulations as may be agreed upon by the supervisory committee and ratified by the court should naturally be inserted in the new instrument of *waqf*. A review procedure may be instituted and it would seem advisable that the court decision should be open to appeal to a higher court, or a special bench of the supreme court, that may review the initial decision and issue a final decision, or indeed order a fresh inquiry if it deems this necessary and advisable. This is only a broad outline of the proceedings that might be involved. Specific details and procedural guidelines may need to be formulated and made available, to be applied on a uniform basis at the national level and possibly also internationally.

As for the assets of *waqf*, the Ḥanafīs have specified that only real property and its attachments, such as tools and animals, and also movable goods that are accepted by prevailing custom, may be assigned as *waqf*. The majority (*jumhūr*) has held, however, that movable assets may be assigned into *waqf* absolutely and references are made in this context to tools, furniture and equipment that makes a mosque or a charitable property functional, as well as books, clothes and weapons regardless of whether they are attached to real property or exist independently—these are all admissible and may be assigned into *waqf*. The *jumhūr* position here is evidently open and comprehensive, and bears great harmony with the spirit of charitable works, which need not be too restrictive, and should not preclude movable goods from the purview of *waqf*. There is little doubt that both the majority (*jumhūr*) and the Ḥanafīs have preferred real property and durable assets to be assigned into *waqf*, and this should still remain the normative position which accords with the assignment in perpetuity and permanent character of *waqf*. If one considers this to be the normal rule, or one that is in harmony with systematic reasoning (*qiyās*), movable goods and assets may be admitted in *waqf* by way of *istiḥsān*, which represents an exception to the normal position. The proposed *istiḥsān* here is not new in fact, and what has been said really repeats the scholastic *istiḥsān* of the Ḥanafī school itself. It is merely proposed that the idea of movable goods should not be given a restrictive interpretation, and may well include assets that are not attached to real property or even assets that have no physical utility or existence. Stocks and shares, unit trusts and partnership capital in companies and corporations that operate in legitimate lines of trade and enjoy permanent status should be admissible in *waqf*. It would seem eminently suitable, for example, to establish a *waqf* corporation that might take up business enterprises in manufacturing, construction, food industries and so forth, and realises revenues that can be utilised for charitable, educational purposes, scientific research and fields of activity which are all too familiar to the history of *waqf* in the not too distant past. While I do not propose to admit perishable goods into the assets of *waqf*, there is no reason why a *waqf* corporation should not be active in food production and processing. But one may need to add here that a portfolio of stocks in another company may fall under the category of movable goods, yet a *waqf* corporation or charitable foundation may well be considered immovable. So movable and immovable assets may be, and indeed should be, considered open categories, and the scope of the proposed *istiḥsān* may also be deemed to be open to new developments.

A general observation that may be made here is that the terms of the *waqf* deed and stipulations that might have been made by the *wāqif* should prevail in all of what has been proposed above. Whether the context is one of declaring a *waqf* revocable, or of re-channelling the assets of *waqf* in a different direction, or of investing them into certain lines of trade that do not belong to the real property sector and so forth—the wishes of the *wāqif* should be followed and considered as far as possible. Should there be specific instructions in the deed of *waqf*, they should be upheld, and failing that, the wishes of the beneficiaries of *waqf*, especially in the case of a private *waqf*, should be ascertained and upheld. Although what is being said here mainly relates to the public (*awqāf khayriyyah*) as opposed to private *waqf* (*awqāf ahliyyah*), our proposals do not necessarily preclude the latter, especially in cases of long-standing private endowments whose beneficiaries might be unknown or have passed away. In that eventuality the private *waqf* also joins the public or charitable category, and may then be treated on the same footing as a public *waqf*. The decision to declare the change of status of a *waqf* holding from a private into a public *waqf* should also be a matter for the court to consider. In some countries like Syria and Egypt, private *awqāf* have been abolished and public *waqf* is the only type of *waqf* that remains valid under the laws promulgated in 1949 and 1952 respectively. This was due mainly to legal complications that arose over the ownership and objectives of *waqf*, and this is why what is proposed here is of relevance primarily to public *awqāf*.

With reference to Muslim minority communities and the status of *awqāf* or other charities therein, this author would argue that an international *awqāf* commission should be set up within the framework of the OIC. This should be done on the recommendation of member countries who should in the meantime authorise a preparatory report on the membership and jurisdiction of the proposed commission and other related matters. The commission should include Sharīʿah specialists among its members and should have judicial powers in the affairs of charities, unclaimed and unowned properties and *waqf*, along similar lines to those of a Sharīʿah court. The OIC governing body should in the meantime explore the possibilities of entering treaty relations with host countries and come up with formulas to enable the *awqāf* commission to make decisions with regard to charities and heirless estates left behind by a member of the minority Muslim community. In the event of there being a sizeable minority, it may be possible to set up a local committee for similar purposes to liase with the *awqāf* commission. Details of this proposal will also have to be worked out and determined in line with the degree of co-operation and support between the OIC member countries and government authorities that have jurisdiction over the Muslim minority in question.

When there is a plan and a well-considered framework for co-operation, it is hoped that there will be all-round support for it.

Efforts should in all cases be made to target local welfare objectives in the utilisation of charities. To make a local charity foundation or *waqf* self-sustaining and profitable, there may be occasion for international co-operation and involvement of the *awqāf* commission, or a standing committee thereof, which would hopefully receive support from the national governments concerned.

A point was made earlier as to ascertaining the will and instructions of the dedicator *wāqif* in all matters of concern to *waqf* that are discussed here. Should there be a stipulation in the *waqf* deed, or where the will of the *wāqif* can be understood and ascertained by other means of evidence, this should be facilitated. In the event, however, when this is not possible, especially when the *waqf* in question dates back over a long period of time, then charitable and pious contribution may be deemed to be the overriding purpose of all public *awqāf*. Should there be need for further specification of the objectives of *waqf* in individual cases, the local judge or the *awqāf* commission, as the case may be, should determine this by way of *istiḥsān*. Here we distinguish the normal rule in regard to determining the purpose of *waqf* to be to refer this to the will and instruction of the *wāqif*, but when this is not feasible or seems doubtful, then the judge or the *awqāf* commission should specify it by way of exceptional *istiḥsān* that may be based on necessity and *maṣlaḥah*. The effective cause (*ʿillah*) of this *istiḥsān* may be said to be the promotion of charity and the effective utilisation of the *waqf* property in line with the true intentions of the *wāqif*.

NOTES

1. Hashmi, 'Management of Waqf: Past and Present,' in Islamic Research and Training Institute, *Management and Development of Waqf*, p. 26.

2. Ibid., p. 26.

3. Ibid.

4. Al-Zarqā, 'Some Modern Means for the Financing and Investment of *Awqāf* Projects,' in IRTI, *Management*, p. 48.

5. Cf. Hassan Amin, '*Waqf* in Islamic Jurisprudence', in IRTI, *Management and Development of Awqāf*, pp. 15-19, and 73.

6. Ibid, p. 74.

7. See for details Ḥassan Amin, 'al-Waqf fi'l-Fiqh,' in ed. Hassan Amin, *Idārah Wa Tathmīr*, p. 108 ff.

8. See for details Muṣṭafā al-Zarqā, *Sharīʿahl-Qawāʿid al-Fiqhiyyah*, p. 179 and 207.

9. Cf. Al-Zuḥaylī, *Al-Fiqh al-Islāmī*, IV, 153; Amin, 'Al-Waqf,' n. 121, p. 96.

CHAPTER ELEVEN

Issues in Islamic Banking

I. Introductory Remarks

Ever since their inception in the early 1970s, Islamic banks have justified their existence and distinguished themselves by their commitment to interest-free banking, and the promotion of equity financing and partnership. These are undoubtedly admirable objectives as they integrate social welfare with the fabric of financial activity and business enterprise. The fact that Islamic banking has made impressive progress within a relatively short period of time must to a large extent be due to the public appeal of its basic philosophy and objectives. Yet aspiring to the ideals of advancing economic justice and being able to promote this and offer a credible alternative to conventional banking in a period of history that can perhaps be described as one of economic Darwinism is fraught with challenges. To be even moderately successful in the face of unequal competition is a notable achievement, and the essential merit and credibility of Islamic banking, that was until recently open to questions, is no longer in doubt. The proliferation of Islamic banks and banking counters in both Muslim and non-Muslim countries has boosted confidence in and the credibility of the system to an unprecedented level. In this evolutionary process, however, the inner mechanisms of Islamic banking have been put to the test on various fronts, especially in regard to the modes of *riba*-free transactions which the banks have been able to offer over the years.

Five modes of transaction, namely partnership (*mushārakah*), commenda partnership (*muḍārabah*), deferred payment sale (*bayᶜ al-*

mu'ajjal) or (*bay*ᶜ *bi-thaman ājil*), profit added sale (*murābaḥah*), and leasing (*ijārah*) lie at the centre stage of the whole idea of Islamic banking. There are other contracts known both to Islamic law and current Islamic banking practices, in the areas especially of co-operative finance and agriculture, but these have, however, been only practised on a limited scale. The benevolent loan (*qarḍ ḥasan*) formula has been utilised in social welfare and educational projects such as the setting up of scholarship-loan schemes for students or providing initial sums of investment funds to help the needy and the unemployed to earn a living. These are worthwhile endeavours which can only look to a better future in tandem with progress and success in the profitable commercial operations of the Islamic financial institutions. The five modes of transaction mentioned above are basically versatile and can accommodate the bulk of the commercial needs and customer requirements of the Islamic banks. They have often been employed and developed in innovative ways in order to diversify banking operations within the given framework of the Sharīᶜah and also to utilise the available opportunities that the market may offer from time to time. All this is, however, driven by the basic goal of making these transactions profitable for the banks, their customers and partners. Variations on the themes of the five principal modes of transaction have sometimes led to a merger of more than one formula as a way of providing a preferable alternative to an existing method, and there is scope for further development along similar lines. The success and dynamism of Islamic banking has often been said to depend on innovation and diversity so as to make banking transactions more versatile and appealing to a wider cross-section of customers, including non-Muslims.

Some of the challenging questions that have arisen so far in countries like Egypt, Pakistan, Iran and Malaysia, where Islamic banks have originated and taken root include the following: firstly, that Islamic banks have tended to avoid taking risk and often devoted their resources to safer modes of financing, or else that they have modified and manipulated existing modes of transaction in various ways so as to transfer commercial risk mainly to the customer. They have as a result heavily relied on *murābaḥah*, *ijārah* and *bay*ᶜ *bi-thaman ājil* and have been reluctant to enter the more risk-oriented modes of *muḍārabah* and *mushārakah* financing. After the initial but limited enthusiasm for *muḍārabah* and partnership financing shown in the relevant statistics until the early 1980s, *muḍārabah* and *mushārakah* transactions have shown a steady decline. In the case of Bank

Islam Malaysia Berhad (BIMB), for example, *muḍārabah* financing represented 3.1 per cent of the total transactions for 1984, but then in the years 1985-1991 declined to less than one per cent. In the case of partnership financing (*mushārakah*), the corresponding figures were 1.2 per cent for 1984, 2.2 per cent for 1986 and then 0.01 per cent in 1991.

The BIMB experience of the 1980s showed the bulk of bank transactions to be in favour of *bayᶜ bi-thaman ājil* and *murābaḥah* financing modes. The former claimed a share of about 50 per cent of transactions in 1984, which rose to about 79 per cent in 1987 and then declined slightly to 73.7 per cent in 1991. This is followed by *murābaḥah,* which declined from an early high of 37 per cent to about 15 per cent and 13 per cent for 1987 and 1991 respectively. And lastly leasing (*ijārah*) transactions accounted for 9.3 per cent of bank financing in 1984, but the figure went down to about 3 per cent in 1988 and rose again to 13 per cent in 1991. There has been no significant change in these patterns ever since.[1]

Secondly, the bulk of Islamic banking transactions have to date consisted of short-term financing in the areas mainly of deferred payment sale, *murābaḥah* and leasing. There is a marked reluctance in the banks' commitment to long-term partnership financing in the areas of *muḍārabah* and *mushārakah.* This is related to the risk-taking element in that long-term financing involves higher risk. The reluctance here has also been due partly to lack of expertise and qualified personnel to carry out efficient project evaluation. The BIMB figures show that in 1992 the larger advances were for housing purchases, land acquisition and construction, and the smaller amounts for manufacturing and trade.[2]

Over two thirds of the BIMB financing was in the form of *bayᶜ bi-thaman ājil* in which the bank typically financed the purchase of goods on behalf of clients who later repaid the bank at an agreed mark-up. The deferment period for the payment was typically one to three months—similar to the period for trade credit from conventional commercial banks. In the case of *murābaḥah* financing, the BIMB actually purchased the goods on behalf of the client and then resold them to the client with a mark-up, repayable typically in three or six months time.[3]

This focus on short-term trade financing is a cause for concern for two main reasons: (1) It is likely to relegate the Islamic banks to the periphery of the financial system. It will attract only a certain type of clientele, much like finance companies in hire-purchase financing or savings and loans for home mortgages. Without taking the centre stage, Islamic banks run the risk of being marginalised. Second, short-term trade financing is largely concerned with the financing of goods already produced, and not with the creation or increase of production capital or with facilities like factories and plants, infrastructure etc. Yet it is investment in such facilities that encourages real economic growth. Hence the current emphasis of Islamic banks on short-term financing is not congruent either with the long term objective of the banks or with their social welfare agenda.[4]

A closer look at some of the financial modes, including jointly managed financing *muḍārabah*, participatory *muḍārabah* (*shibh al-muḍārabah*), *muḍārabah* and mark-up, profit added sale *murābaḥah* and partnership financing *mushārakah*, may throw light on some of these issues.

II. Jointly-Managed Muḍārabah

The Islamic banking experiences of Malaysia, Egypt and Pakistan indicate that the idea of equity financing and partnership, a vital part of the basic philosophy of Islamic banking, has in practice not been fully realised. This is partly due to the cautious attitude the banks have taken toward risk-sharing and also towards medium and long-term investment. The declining trend in the use of *muḍārabah* and *mushārakah* is a result also of the limitations that the banks have encountered in their dealings with customers and partners. It has been observed that honesty and trust, being the necessary ingredients of successful partnership, have unfortunately not been typical of entrepreneurs who have associated with the bank. People do not always declare their profits and assets, and if they do, they tend to manipulate facts and such experiences do not help the banks to venture out and encourage the *mushārakah* and *muḍārabah* financing modes. With reference to the Bank Islam Malaysia for instance, one observer noted that 'the Bank had been cheated by some of its customers in the past. Some of them did not declare their profits, while others did not possess the skill to participate in business.'[5]

Another contributory factor to this scenario is the established rule of the *fiqh* of *muḍārabah*, which disentitles the owner of capital, the Islamic bank, for example, when it acts as financier (*rabb al-māl*), to play an active role in the management of the *muḍārabah* assets. The normal rules of *fiqh* in other words do not allow the financier to participate in, or supervise, the activities of the entrepreneur (*muḍārib*).

But in recent times it has been felt that when the bank provides the capital, it should also have a role in the management of the project and the utilisation of the *muḍārabah* capital.[6] Certain changes have evidently occurred over time which might have a bearing on the effectiveness of the original rules of *muḍārabah* and their application to real situations now. At a time when there were no corporations and companies of scale, the rules of *fiqh* contemplated person to person relations and the element of trust that could easily be identified in that context. But under the present circumstances when the world of business and finance has become almost totally impersonal and dominated by giant corporations, each pursuing a complex mix of policies and objectives, one wonders how effective the original rulings of *muḍārabah* can be in this situation. Perhaps we have here a case for recourse to a *maṣlaḥah*-inspired *istiḥsān* which might enable us to make a suitable exception to the normal rules of *muḍārabah*, and consequently allow the financier to take part in the management of *muḍārabah* capital.

Our attempt here might be criticised in that instead of trying to alter the contract of *muḍārabah*, it might be better to create a new contract, such as the profit and loss sharing contract that has for similar reasons been introduced in Pakistan. The PLS contract was initially designed as a substitute to *muḍārabah* but was called by a different name so as to be known as a new contract. In this contract the owner of the capital is assigned a participatory role in the operation and progress of the project. Gamal Attia has explained that when the preparatory committee for the Islamisation of the economy in Pakistan took up the issue, they preferred to avoid coming under the rules of the traditional *muḍārabah* contract and developed a scheme of profit and loss sharing finance under which the same kind of finance as a *muḍārabah* is offered with the only difference that the bank can take part and intervene in the management and control of the project.[7] But for reasons that are explained below it is not proposed here to introduce a new contract but only a modified variety of the familiar *muḍārabah*.

By offering the jointly-managed *muḍārabah* variation, the Islamic bank can contribute towards the success of the venture by making available its institutional expertise to the *muḍārib* and also prevent the prospects of financial mismanagement and loss. The choice of applying *istiḥsān* to this situation has not been exercised and no one seems to have raised the possibility. One of the advantages of recourse to *istiḥsān* in this situation, as indeed in all cases where *istiḥsān* can properly apply, would be that *istiḥsān* merely advises an appropriate exception to the normal rules without actually proposing to interfere with or to nullify those rules. When we make an exception to an aspect of *muḍārabah*, for example, we propose to leave intact the normal specifications of this contract, which would mean that the bank can still offer, if it considers it appropriate, the normal *muḍārabah*, and also to have a modified version of the same and apply it when it seems to be of benefit. We are in other words not proposing to replace the *muḍārabah* or even to change its original rules but only to make a suitable exception. The fear of mismanagement and loss, which is the effective cause (*ʿillah*) of the proposed *istiḥsān*, must be present so as to justify recourse to jointly-managed *muḍārabah*. When this fear is absent and the *rabb al-māl* or the Islamic bank has no cause for concern about mismanagement and financial loss, then the normal *muḍārabah* would be applicable and should be available as a matter of choice. To introduce this adjustment may help revitalise the declining *muḍārabah* mode of financing and give it the place it merits in the transaction portfolio of Islamic banks.

The *istiḥsān* I have proposed here applies mainly to cases where one of the parties to *muḍārabah* is an institution, such as the Islamic bank, and not a private individual, as would probably be the case in the prototype contract of *muḍārabah*. This is mainly to do, as I explained earlier, with the question of fiduciary relations which occur somewhat differently between two individuals and between an individual and an organisation. The organisation which is entering a *muḍārabah* contract with an individual entrepreneur should consequently be able to take part in the management of *muḍārabah*, initially at least, but should have the choice to convert to the prototype whenever that model might seem more appropriate.

III. The *Muḍārabah* Look-Alike *(Shibh al-Muḍārabah)*

Whereas the jointly-managed *muḍārabah* seeks to enhance the participatory role of the financier (*rab al-māl*), *shibh al-muḍārabah* aims to enhance the participatory role of the entrepreneur or *muḍārib*. Both these models in turn promote risk-sharing and joint liability between the *muḍārabah* partners. The proposal here also serves the purpose of introducing diversity into the operational modes of this transaction. The idea here is to entitle the entrepreneur to acquire a stake in the operational capital of *muḍārabah*. When the *muḍārib* has a share in the capital, he will also be entitled to a portion of the profit in addition to what he would normally be entitled to receive on account of his labour, management and skill. This manner of adjustment may not be entirely acceptable to the theory of *muḍārabah* as it involves the transfer of liability for loss at least partially to the *muḍārib*. Be that as it may, *shibh al-muḍārabah* does warrant attention because of the declining role of *muḍārabah* in Islamic banking. *Shibh al-muḍārabah* represents a cross between *muḍārabah* and *mushārakah* as it partakes of the attributes of both and introduces to them an element of flexibility, and at the same time enhances the partnership component of *muḍārabah*. It also offers the advantage of enhancing involvement and co-operation, especially in the event where the *muḍārib* possesses expertise and can contribute to the operational capital. The partner-cum-*muḍārib* who may be an expert in the field and volunteers to risk his own assets would by doing so to inspire confidence. *Shibh al-muḍārabah* could provide a partial remedy to the existing situation where the Islamic bank often turns down a *muḍārabah* project because of reluctance to be the only financier in a venture it may know little about, where it cannot trust the credentials of the entrepreneur. The formula discussed here should not necessarily be disagreeable to the existing rules of *muḍārabah*, which is itself a form of partnership, and the terms of that partnership may well comprise elements of *muḍārabah* and *mushārakah*. Having said this, however, the jurists of the leading schools of *fiqh* have spoken against risk-sharing and the transfer of liability for loss to the *muḍārib*. This, according to the *fiqh* rules, should be the sole responsibility of the capital provider, *rabb al-māl*. But it seems that the jurists have spoken against the transfer of risk in a total sense to the *muḍārib*, which is not proposed here. The partial transfer of risk in our proposal is justified to the extent that the *muḍārib* participates in the capital of *muḍārabah*.

In some cases the *muḍārib* may persuade the bank to grant him a benevolent loan for the purpose of raising an investment fund, while in other cases the *muḍārib* may be in a position to provide tangible assets, machinery and equipment that might be essential for the project. To offer a blend between *muḍārabah* and *mushārakah* would help to diffuse the risk-taking element of *muḍārabah* by transferring a part of that risk from the financier to the *muḍārib*, and help to make *muḍārabah* a more attractive proposition from the viewpoints of both the entrepreneur and the Islamic bank.

IV. *Muḍārabah* and Mark-Up

Muḍārabah can be further diversified by attempting to amalgamate *muḍārabah* and *murābaḥah* in that the latter can be inserted as a stipulation of the *muḍārabah* agreement. The owner of capital (*rabb al-māl*) and the entrepreneur may thus agree that sales and purchases incurred as part of the *muḍārabah* activities must be on a *murābaḥah* basis. This would mean that the entrepreneur declares not only the profit made but also the prices of sales and purchases, which would bring visibility to the contents of *muḍārabah* and serve, in turn, as a confidence-building measure between the owner and entrepreneur.[8] The owner of the capital can also specify in advance the sale price and the profit margin that is to be realised, and instruct the *muḍārib* accordingly. This information would also have to be declared, according to the requirements of *murābaḥah*, to the third party, that is, the buyer, and enable the latter to make a considered choice about the purchase. This amendment to the *muḍārabah* prototype can be justified on the basis of *istiḥsān* that is predicated on benefit *maṣlaḥah*, in that we need to open up the scope of *muḍārabah* so as to ensure its viability in the operational modes of Islamic banking. The proposed *istiḥsān* involves a partial departure, or an exception, to the established rules of *muḍārabah* in favour of an alternative that seems preferable in the interest of introducing diversity to Islamic Banking operations. The specific rule of *muḍārabah*, which is abandoned in the proposed model, is that instead of merely specifying a formula for the division of the contract, the *muḍārib* specifies the component elements of that profit, namely the purchase price and the mark up on sales. The effective cause (*ʿillah*) of the proposed *istiḥsān* may be said to be an enhancement of visibility in the operational terms of *muḍārabah* that would promote objectivity and confidence in the terms of this contract. As it is *muḍārabah* that is marginalised, it does not find the level of support it merits in the transaction portfolio of Islamic banks, partly because of doubts about the credibility and prudence of the *muḍārib* and the financial viability of his entrepreneurial activities. The proposed amalgamation between *muḍārabah* and *murābaḥah* would help to allay some of the fears that are bound to arise at the initial stages of concluding a *muḍārabah* contract, especially when it involves undertaking new business ventures with prospects that may not have been known to the market.

Our proposed variation of the terms of *muḍārabah* may not be acceptable to the established rules of *muḍārabah*, which tend to leave the *muḍārib* at liberty in the matter of sales and purchases, and admit no restriction or supervision on his freedom to determine the details of the trade himself. Part of the reason for this is that the entrepreneur acts in the capacity both of representative (*wakīl*) and trustee (*amīn*), and giving specific instruction to the *muḍārib* is deemed to be disagreeable to his capacity as trustee. But a departure is still proposed from this position by recourse to exceptional *istiḥsān*.

A question may arise as to why one needs to attempt the suggested amalgamation between *muḍārabah* and *murābaḥah* within the framework of *istiḥsān*, and not as it were by way of making a reasonable suggestion under the aegis of unrestricted reasoning (*istidlāl mursal*), or even *maṣlaḥah*?

In response it may be argued that approaching the issue from the perspective of *istiḥsān* would imply that one only suggests a limited amendment/departure from the existing *fiqhī* framework of *muḍārabah*. The Islamic bank may make the proposed combination available as a matter of choice, that is, side by side with the original *muḍārabah*. The other advantage of approaching the issue from the perspective of *istiḥsān* is that *istiḥsān*, like *qiyās*, operates on the basis of an identifiable effective cause (*ᶜillah*), at least according to the view taken by many prominent Ḥanafī jurists. To identify the basic *ᶜillah* and rationale of the proposed transaction would help to give it identity and character, and it may also help the parties, especially the Islamic financial institution, towards the proper application of the amalgamated version. As for the question raised over *maṣlaḥah*, it may be explained that the *istiḥsān* proposed here is based on *maṣlaḥah* and this provides a partial answer to the question I have posed. The basic purpose is, of course, to secure *maṣlaḥah*, yet I would still argue that *istiḥsān* is a more appropriate framework from the viewpoint of the particularisation of *ᶜillah*. *Maṣlaḥah* is open ended and does not, as we note from the manner it is treated in *uṣūl al-fiqh*,[9] require identification of a particular *ᶜillah*. But since *istiḥsān* proposes a departure from the existing rules, it must be based on a particular *ᶜillah*—and hence my approach to the issue through the perspective of *istiḥsān*.

V. *Murābaḥah*

Murābaḥah and its related mark-up procedure involve two sales transactions with an agreed mark-up on the original price in the second sale. For example, a client might suggest that his bank purchases certain goods such as a machine, raw materials or trade merchandise. The bank buys the goods on its own account from a supplier, selling it on to the client at a previously agreed marked-up price. The mark-up contains the cost the bank incurred in its services as well as a profit margin. The transaction is labeled *murābaḥah* unless the goods are delivered on the spot with payment deferred in instalments, in which case it would be called *bay*ᶜ *mu'ajjal*, or *bay*ᶜ *bi-thaman ājil*.

Commenting on the somewhat distorted practice of *murābaḥah* in Pakistan, Gieraths wrote that the basic difference between the mark-up and interest is that the former is theoretically linked to a real goods transaction and the latter to a financial transaction. But when the bank avoids any participation in a real goods transaction, it forfeits the claim that it is performing *bay*ᶜ *mu'ajjal* or *murābaḥah*. In practice, 'even fictitious transactions, existing only on contract paper, are made use of to back up credit transactions on a mark-up basis.'[10] This is especially common in personal loans: the supplier and bank client are the same person. The client sells an item to the bank, for example his car, and buys it back at a mark-up price. The bank authorises him to continue to use the car, while the payment is deferred and made in instalments. The mark-up procedure has thus been criticised on the following points:

(a) Banks do not handle the goods.

(b) Mark-up is calculated on a time-related scale.

(c) The risk involved in holding the goods is borne by the client throughout the transaction.

It is then stated that in the vast majority of cases mark-up has substituted what was formerly known as interest, working in a remarkably similar way 'following the letter of the Islamic injunction but hardly its spirit.'[11]

Attia wrote that the difference between *murābaḥah* and the interest bearing loan is legal rather than economic. The detailed justification of *murābaḥah* as it is practised by the Islamic banks depends on the degree of risk that they take in financing a commercial transaction. The risk involved here is also represented mainly by the time lag between the purchase of goods by the bank and their resale to the customer. If this period is long enough to expose the bank to a risk, then there is a real difference between this scheme and the interest bearing loan and the bank is justified in adding a profit margin to its cost in proportion to the risk it is undertaking. But when the purchase and sale are completed simultaneously, as is now often the case, in such a way that the risk element is minimised for the bank, this mere formality without substance does not justify the application of *murābaḥah*.[12]

In an attempt to prevent distortion in the market practices of *murābaḥah*, one needs to look towards measures that would encourage risk-sharing and partnership between the parties and this can be done partly perhaps by synthesizing *murābaḥah* with partnership *mushārakah*. The parties to a *murābaḥah* sale may be permitted to engage in buying and selling on a partnership basis. Two or more persons can thus jointly buy the commodity they wish to trade, and share the profit that is accrued from the mark-up sale in proportion to their share in the initial capital in accordance with the terms of a previous agreement. The losses are, however, to be apportioned, in all circumstances, on the basis of the parties' share in the capital.[13] This may take the form where the customer who has expert knowledge of a certain commodity or line of trading approaches the bank to purchase certain goods on a *murābaḥah*-cum-partnership basis, in which case the bank will be acting not as the owner but a partner and trustee, and will jointly purchase and sell on a *murābaḥah* basis, and then divide the profit in accordance with the terms of their previous agreement. This would also mean that both parties will share responsibility (*ḍamān*) for storage, safe-keeping and other expenses that are incurred as a result.

An alternative mode of the same transaction would be that the client who approaches the bank owns the goods or merchandise in question and asks the bank to enter into a partnership with him and utilise the bank's expertise and resources in marketing and other aspects of the trade. As soon as there is an agreement, the parties must specify their respective share in the capital and agree on the apportionment of the profit. The partnership should be based on a real transaction and not on a credit basis as this might give rise to the possibility of *ribā*, especially if there is a time lag between the partnership agreement and the eventual *murābaḥah* sale.

The above-mentioned eventualities obviously assume a *murābaḥah*-based partnership in which the bank and the individual sell their jointly-owned commodity to a third party. But when the trader himself is the purchaser and the bank acts as the seller of *murābaḥah*, in this situation the parties can also enter a partnership and conclude the purchase on that basis. This may, in turn, be followed by a second transaction in which one of the partners becomes the seller and the other becomes the buyer on the basis of *murābaḥah*. This can obviously be done after the conclusion of the initial purchase, and the precise determination of each party's share in the capital. The sale price is then determined by reference to the market price in the locality or preferably by reference to a previously agreed formula, and if there is a profit involved in the second sale, it should also be divided according to the terms of a prior agreement or the respective share of the parties in the initial investment.

This variation on the original theme of *murābaḥah* evidently involves a certain departure from the prototype to a synthesis between *murābaḥah* and *mushārakah*, and the formula involved here may be said to be in the nature of *istiḥsān* that is predicated on *maṣlaḥah*. The basic *maṣlaḥah* here is to prevent distortion in the practice of *murābaḥah*, which often turns it into a thinly-disguised interest-bearing loan. To integrate *mushārakah* within the fabric of *murābaḥah* involves a departure from the rules of *murābaḥah*. For *murābaḥah* is a variety of sale which does not involve partnership or a mixing of assets between the buyer and seller. Yet *murābaḥah* and *mushārakah* do have one aspect in common which is that both are fiduciary contracts and require the parties involved to reveal all the material facts of the trade to one another. The *istiḥsān* that is attempted here proceeds on the basis of a particular effective cause (*ʿillah*), which is the sharing or apportioning of liability for destruction and loss (*ḍamān*).

The whole purpose of a *murābaḥah* sale is to realise a profit, and the basic guideline of Sharīʿah pertaining to this position is that profit follows *ḍamān*: one who is entitled to a profit must also take part in the liability for destruction and loss—hence the proposed *ʿillah* for the partnership-based *murābaḥah*. The proposal here is once again in the nature of a partial departure from, or an exception, to the prototype *murābaḥah*, which should remain available in its original form, and the departure to the new format that is proposed here may be attempted only when its basic rationale and *ʿillah* is present. In the original *fiqhī* formula of *murābaḥah*, liability for loss (*ḍamān*) rests with the seller, but our proposed model is based on the rationale that in their capacities as partners, both parties will have a stake in the capital and also share responsibility for destruction and loss. Some of the detailed aspects of the parties' relationship in the *murābaḥah* especially with regard to the question of what is counted as profit and what is part of the capital are regulated in the *fiqh* rules of *murābaḥah*, and our proposal here assumes that they remain applicable. The *fiqh* rules on many of these issues refer the matter to prevailing custom which is especially held to be applicable in the absence of a contractual agreement between the parties. Our basic concern with the integrity of *murābaḥah*, and with its proposed modification here, is to keep both clear of credit-based *ribā* (*ribā al-nasi'ah*) and also of unwarranted uncertainty (*gharar*) that may amount to one party taking unfair advantage of the other.

VI. *Mushārakah*

Mushārakah is a partnership between two or more persons, all of whom have a share in the finance, and one or more parties are responsible for entrepreneurship and management. Profits are shared in previously agreed proportions while losses are borne in proportion to the respective shares in the total capital.

A client wishing to do business with a bank on a *mushārakah* basis has to provide extensive data for the bank on entrepreneurial results, balances, profit and loss records and project specifications and prospects. Banks are usually reluctant to enter into long-term commitments and would rather finance quick profit generating projects than long term projects, because even though the latter might be more profitable, they take longer to mature and bear higher risks. On average, low-profit, low-risk projects are preferred to high profit, high-risk ones. The client's behaviour follows similar patterns: clients promoting low-risk-projects will rather strive for mark-up financing facilities with a fixed cost of capital instead of sharing their low-risk project in a *mushārakah* arrangement. Banks are thus more likely to be offered risky projects for *mushārakah* contracts, as the absence of a fixed cost of capital works as an incentive to such offers.[14]

As already noted, the main issue in *mushārakah* financing has to do with risk-sharing. There is on the one hand a tendency that clients typically propose risky projects for *mushārakah* financing to the Islamic bank, and they are reluctant, on the other hand, to enter *mushārakah* agreements when they are assured of the profitable prospects of their projects. The last thing the Islamic bank wants to do, if the project is not successful, is to share the losses. This would partly explain why *mushārakah* financing, although central to the philosophy of Islamic banking, has not been an active area of Islamic banking transactions. As a mode of finance, *mushārakah* has in the past applied only to well-managed and reliable businesses and institutions, and not so much to setting up venture capital in risk-oriented projects. The challenge really lies in finding acceptable methods by which to reconcile the different interests of the banks and their clients in *mushārakah* transactions.

A method consisting of bonus payment for good management has been introduced in Pakistan which is a matter of agreement between the parties when the *mushārakah* document is being drawn. The bank expects the client to project a profit margin in the *mushārakah* and then the two sides agree on the method of its apportionment. A specified minimum profit is forecast based on past record and available information. The main reason for this is to ensure that the bank does not enter into an agreement if the company has any doubt as to the profitability of the proposed *mushārakah*. When the time comes the bank receives its portion in the profit but if there is greater profit than expected, that is paid back to the company by way of bonuses for good management of the *mushārakah*.[15] But if the company does not pay back the bank is entitled to the shares of the company equalling the amount of loss incurred by the bank. In this way the bank limits its loss (and also its profit) in the *mushārakah* but ensures that the client does not seek bank participation in a bad project. The method has, however, been criticised in that it tends to defy the essence of *mushārakah* as it tends to fall short of a genuine risk-sharing partnership.[16]

The problem of debt repayment in *mushārakah* financing can be more troublesome in the context of Islamic finance as the Islamic bank cannot impose interest on late payment. To address this issue it has been suggested that there should be a penalty clause in the *mushārakah* agreement which should apply in the event of default by a capable debtor and the exact amount should be decided either by a special committee or court.[17] The reason is, of course, that people should not be allowed to delay in performance and not have to pay for it. While creditors are instructed in the clear text of the Qur'ān (al-Baqarah, 2:280) to give grace periods to debtors in difficulty, default by a debtor who is able to pay is oppression and injustice on the authority of an equally explicit ḥadīth and the defaulter may therefore be penalised for it.

These are some of the remedies that have either been tried or suggested to overcome the difficulties of *mushārakah* financing, which are admittedly half solutions and on the whole do not address the issue directly. These may still be useful but the measures that are taken are remedial rather than preventive and there is scope for different measures that address the contractual terms of *mushārakah*, I propose that one way of doing this is to synthesise *mushārakah* with *murābaḥah*.

In the discussion of *murābaḥah* earlier, a merger of *murabaḥah* and *mushārakah* was proposed for the purpose mainly of risk-sharing and participation. The issue here is basically the same, which is why I once again propose a blend between *mushārakah* and *murābaḥah*. The main difference to note here is that the basic framework for our present proposal is *mushārakah*, and a partial departure from its established prototype in *fiqh* is suggested in favour of *murābaḥah*. Hence we presume that the rules of *fiqh* that govern *mushārakah* will still apply to our proposed model. The basic idea is to promote transparency within the terms of *mushārakah* that will eventually cast light on the risk-sharing aspect of *mushārakah*. Although *mushārakah* does mean risk-sharing, the problem is to do with credibility and the true intentions of the parties that propose to enter a *mushārakah* agreement. This is to some extent a question of visibility, and the adoption of measures to ensure that the expressed intention is also manifested in the contractual terms of the proposed partnership.

To integrate *murābaḥah* within the framework of *mushārakah* would enable the parties to stipulate in their *mushārakah* contract that all sales and purchases on behalf of the partnership must be conducted on a *murābaḥah* basis. This would imply that there has to be complete openness with regard to prices and profit or loss, as the case may be, and that the slightest concealment or distortion of facts would amount to a breach of the fiduciary relations on which both *murābaḥah* and partnership are founded. Whenever an individual or a company proposes a project, a business venture or a line of trade on a *mushārakah* basis to the Islamic bank, the bank will naturally solicit as much information as it can on the feasibility and merit of the project, and the credit-worthiness of the proposed partner. When the prospects appear positive the bank may stipulate in the proposed *mushārakah* that sales and purchases on behalf of the partnership should be on a *murābaḥah* basis. Since the parties to a *mushārakah* are agent (*wakīl*) and trustee (*amīn*) on behalf of one another, the stipulation may only serve as a confidence-building measure and provide a more reliable basis for the proposed partnership.

The only objection that one might expect to this proposal may be that it could be less than agreeable to one of the basic aspects of *mushārakah* in that *mushārakah* requires a total merger of the assets of the partners into a single common pool, so that the component parts of the common fund are no longer distinguishable from one another. This is an aspect of *mushārakah* which also provides the logical basis of another requirement, namely that *mushārakah* must always remain open to the representation (*wakālah*) of each one of the partners representing all the others individually and collectively on behalf of the partnership. Now if the *mushārakah* agreement stipulates total disclosure of trade activities, prices and assets, this may appear somewhat at odds with the terms of trust in *mushārakah*, although there need not be any inherent contradiction. But there is nevertheless a departure from the normal rules of *mushārakah* in our proposal to a *murābaḥah*-based partnership by way of exceptional *istiḥsān* inspired by considerations of *maṣlaḥah*.

The benefit that is hoped to be secured here is to contribute to the success of *ribā*-free banking and, more specifically, to revive the declining *mushārakah* and turn it into a viable proposition. The effective cause of this variation may be said to be to enhance transparency in the terms of *mushārakah*. The Islamic bank that might be acting as financier in a *mushārakah* transaction mode may find that this variation of *mushārakah* provides a more open and relatively more informed basis for the risk-sharing aspect of the transaction at hand. The *istiḥsān* attempted here involves a departure, on an exceptional basis, from the established rules of *mushārakah*, and the model proposed is intended to merely diversify the *mushārakah* format and provide a preferable option when there is a need for it, but it is not intended to replace the prototype *mushārakah*. This is the broad outline of a proposal which may need to be further specified, and a set of rules may be worked out so as to regulate the operational aspects of its implementation.

NOTES

1. Wong Choo Sum, 'Bank Islam Malaysia', in Al-Harran, edr. *Islamic Banking*, pp. 94-96.
2. Al-Harran, ed., *Islamic Banking*, p. 70.
3. Ibid. p. 72.
4. Cf. Bacha, 'Conventional Versus Mudarabah Financing,' *J. of Islamic Economics*, International Islamic University Malaysia.
5. Wong Choo Sum, 'Bank Islam Malaysia', in al-Harran, edr, *Islamic Banking*, p. 96.
6. Cf. Gamal Attia, 'Financial Instruments,' in Butterworths Staff, *Islamic Banking*, p. 113.
7. Ibid.
8. Cf. Al-Baᶜlī, *Asāsiyāt*, p. 85.
9. For details on *maṣlaḥah* see Kamalī 'Have We Neglected the Sharīᶜah Law Doctrine of Maṣlaḥah?' *Islamic Studies*, 27 (1988), 287-305.
10. Gieraths, 'Pakistan: Financial Products,' in Wilson, *Islamic Financial Markets*, pp. 184-185.
11. Ibid, p. 193.
12. Gamal Attia, 'Financial Instruments used by Islamic Banks', in Butterworths Staff, *Islamic Banking*, p. 114.

13. Cf. Al-Ba'lī, *Asāsiyyāt*, p. 81.

14. Cf. Gieraths, Pakistan: 'Financial Products', in Wilson, edr. *Islamic Financial Markets*, p. 187.

15. Cf. Ingram, 'Islamic Banking,' in Butterworths Staff, *Islamic Banking*, p. 62.

16. Cf. Gieraths, n. 132, p. 286.

17. Ingram, n. 137 at 64.

CHAPTER TWELVE

The Issue of Unclaimed Assets

An instance of *istiḥsān* that dates back to the time of Companions may be cited here in conjunction with a parallel situation that has arisen typically in the area of pension funds and other long-term saving accounts. The incident I refer to was one of *maṣlaḥah*- based *istiḥsān* that involved three of the first four caliphs, ʿUmar ibn al-Khaṭṭāb, ʿUthmān ibn ʿAffān and ʿAlī ibn Abī Ṭālib, and one of the leading ʿulamā' among the followers (*tābiʿūn*), Saʿīd ibn al-Musayyib, concerning missing and runaway camels. It has been reported that during the time of the caliph ʿUmar ibn al-Khaṭṭāb, missing camels that were not claimed by anyone were left at large. No one would take them or care for their new-born until the time of the third caliph ʿUthmān, when he issued orders for their identification and assessment, and gave instructions that they should be sold and the revenue given to their owners whenever they claimed their camels. Then there was a change from this during the time of caliph ʿAlī ibn Abī Ṭālib, who issued instruction that these camels to be kept in a separate grazing area and be taken care of out of the funds of the public treasury (*bayt al-māl*). The expenses were to be moderate, enough for the animals to be kept alive until the owners came forward and claimed them. They were to remain there and not to be sold, and Saʿīd ibn al-Musayyib held that this was the preferable solution.[1]

Ibn al-Musayyib's recommendation might have been seen as a preferable course to take at the time but if one were to take one's lead from this precedent and reflect on the issue, for example, of the large amounts of unclaimed funds in the statutory pension fund, known as the Employee Provident Fund (EPF) of Malaysia, or government pension funds in other Muslim countries, one might consider the *istiḥsān* of ʿUthmān ibn ʿAffān to be the most suitable. This question has arisen in Malaysia and the difficulty of choosing a preferable course to take is to a large extent a matter of choosing between the ruling of *qiyās*, or following what would appear to be the normal rule, and that of *istiḥsān*. To resort to *istiḥsān* here would mean to formulate an alternative solution which may be contrary to *qiyās*, but may nevertheless seem more suitable under the circumstances. To follow *qiyās*, one would be inclined to follow the course that was taken by ʿUmar ibn al-Khaṭṭāb, namely that no one should interfere with the property of another person, regardless of any honourable intentions. This would, however, fail to offer a satisfactory solution as it involves a waste of resources and leads to problems with roaming animals that could become a public hazard. The *istiḥsān* that is attributed to the caliph ʿUthmān is preferable on grounds of prudence and also the prevention of waste and hazards. A possible solution for the EPF and other pension funds, where thousands of accounts containing large sums of money remain unclaimed, would be that the funds be invested in the names of their owners and taken care of until they are claimed either by their owners or legal heirs. If in the final analysis, after a hundred years or so they are still unclaimed, they could be transferred to charities, including *awqāf*, in the names of their owners so that it would theoretically be possible to trace their records, but the income from those funds would be utilised by charitable foundations and orphanages and give assistance to the ill and the disabled.

To follow the normal rule, or that of *qiyās*, in this situation would mean that nothing should be done which might amount to interference in the private assets of pensioners and these accounts should remain as they are. This would, however, be less than satisfactory and a departure from the normal rule by way of *istiḥsān* would appear preferable. The effective cause of this *istiḥsān* may be said to be the utilisation of idle resources for charitable purposes and the promotion of a caring society through benevolence and good work.

NOTES

1. Cf. Al-Bājī, *Al-Muntaqā*, VI, 143; Mīqā, *Al-Ra'y*, p. 437.

Conclusion

There is a considerable parity, of both substance and form, between *istiḥsān* and the ends and purposes of Sharīʿah (*maqāṣid al-Sharīʿah*). The basic theme and philosophy of the *maqāṣid al-Sharīʿah* is almost identical with that of *istiḥsān* and I take this opportunity to emphasise one aspect of *istiḥsān* which has not received attention in the conventional treatment of the doctrine. The question I raise here is whether *istiḥsān* can be used as an instrument of consolidation between *uṣūl al-fiqh* and the *maqāṣid*. I shall not delve here into the debate as to how and why the methodological thought of earlier centuries virtually ignored the broader approach to the understanding of Sharīʿah taken by the advocates of the *maqāṣid*, and that it was not until the eighth century Hijrah that al-Shāṭibī developed the theory of the *maqāṣid* and opened a new chapter in the history of Islamic jurisprudence. Unlike the Traditionists (Ahl al-Ḥadīth) and the literalists of the Ẓāhirī school, who took an atomistic and mechanical approach to the understanding of Sharīʿah, the advocates of the *maqāṣid* saw the Sharīʿah as goal-oriented and understood the meaning of scripture in the light of the broader objectives of Sharīʿah. The literalists saw the divine words of the Qur'ān (and Sunnah) as value points in themselves rather than the vehicle for values. The advocates of the *maqāṣid* on the other hand placed greater emphasis on the overall reading of the text and treated the Sharīʿah as an integrated whole. This was in marked contrast to the piecemeal approach of the literalists who confined themselves to the words of a given text at the expense even of the broader philosophy and objectives of the Sharīʿah. This in a nutshell is the basic division which runs through the long history of Islamic jurisprudential thought ever since the emergence of the Ahl al-Ra'y and Ahl al-Ḥadīth in the first century Hijrah. The bifurcation of juristic thought outlined here has in many ways continued to manifest itself in one form or another, not only in the scholastic thoughts of the *madhāhib*, but also the juristic writings and orientations of ᶜulamā' and scholars in more recent times.

Being essentially a manifestation of juristic opinion (*ra'y*), *istiḥsān* lay at the centre of the Ahl al-Ra'y/ Ahl al-Ḥadīth controversy, and the debate about the validity or otherwise of *istiḥsān* has in many ways been lacking in equilibrium. The juristic controversy over *istiḥsān* was somehow unable to clear the grounds and develop the potential of *istiḥsān* into a unified philosophy and outlook. The debate between the Ahl al-Ra'y and Ahl al-Ḥadīth, as we learn from history, drove them to the brink of hostility amidst a plethora of charges and counter-charges that were less than justified and acceptable.

There were efforts on the part of the outstanding ᶜulamā' of the early centuries to try to articulate a unified methodology of *uṣūl al-fiqh* and they were on the whole successful in achieving their purpose. Yet there remained areas where the effort at consolidation and coherence was less successful. This is manifested not only in the Ḥanafī-Shāfiᶜī debate about *istiḥsān* but also the gap that became increasingly obvious in the legal theory of *uṣūl al-fiqh*, on account of its failure to integrate the *maqāṣid al-Sharīᶜah* into the fabric of its methodology. One of the principle architects of this methodology, Imam al-Shāfiᶜī, took a somewhat restrictive attitude to *ra'y* and *ijtihād* and the methodology he articulated for *ijtihād* was in line with this. Unlike the climate of opinion that prevails now, which is decidedly anti-*taqlīd* and pro-*ijtihād*, during al-Shāfiᶜī's time the imposition restrictions on ra'y and *ijtihād* was seen as the preferable course of action to take.

As stated earlier, *istiḥsān* is generic in that its scope covers almost the entire range of the *aḥkām* both in the areas of *muᶜāmalāt* and *ᶜibādāt*, and it seeks, as is evident from its methodology and evidential leanings, to harmonise the detailed rules of Sharīᶜah in line with the broader objectives of the *maqāṣid*. But unlike unregulated *ra'y* or unrestricted reasoning (*istidlāl mursal*), *istiḥsān* seeks to promote these objectives on the strength of valid *sharᶜī* evidence. To secure justice, benefit and *iḥsān* and to find ways of removing and eliminating hardship, as well as accommodating the exigencies of necessity and *ᶜurf*, are at once the common themes and objectives of the *maqāṣid* and *istiḥsān*.

The renewed interest in recent decades that the writers and scholars of Sharīᶜah have taken in the *maqāṣid al-Sharīᶜah* is attested by the publication, in rapid succession, of numerous works, especially in the Arabic language, on the subject. Apart from the intrinsic merit of this theme, the fresh emphasis is partly due to the somewhat restrictive and theoretical orientations of *uṣūl al-fiqh* and its methodology for *ijtihād*, which have not really responded well to the demands of Islamic revivalism and reform. *Uṣūl al-fiqh* has grown in complexity and it is, in any case, not particularly suitable for the age of statutory legislation in which *ijtihād* is not the moving force of legislation, and the *mujtahid* has no recognised status in the legislative machinery of the modern state. The call for the renewal of *ijtihād*, issued about a century ago by al-Afghānī, Muhammad Abduh and others has not, for understandable reasons, generated the momentum that was hoped at one time. I do not say that *uṣūl al-fiqh* has lost its relevance to contemporary issues or to statutory legislation, yet it is by no means an exaggeration to say that neither *ijtihād* nor its methodology, the *uṣūl al-fiqh*, have become an engaging process, a national or an international agenda, as one might have hoped. There is, of course, a renewal of interest at various levels, such as we currently observe in Islamic banking, Islamic universities etc; which is, however, of a specialist kind and can best be seen as part of an evolving picture and still relevant, yet infrastructural, gradualist and piecemeal. Be that as it may, we have seen a considerable surge of academic interest in the *maqāṣid al Sharīᶜah* partly because, I believe, of the difficulties of regenerating *ijtihād* through the formulations of *uṣūl al-fiqh*, and providing a functional methodology for it. The *maqāṣid al-Sharīᶜah* is relatively free of the kind of technicalities that are attended by the various doctrines of *uṣūl al-fiqh* such as *ijmāᶜ*, *qiyās* and *istiḥsān* etc. The manner in which the *maqāṣid* deals with the materials of Sharīᶜah and the way it seeks to utilise the resources of the Qur'ān, Sunnah and *fiqh* is also inherently versatile. This is because as a discipline of Sharīᶜah, the *maqāṣid* is primarily concerned with the ends and objectives of Sharīᶜah rather than conformity to technical details, which seem to be the dominant concern of the various doctrines of *uṣūl al-fiqh*. To be unduly concerned with technical requirements can easily blur one's clarity of vision and purpose at the altar of methodological accuracy and conformity to precedent.

Another facet of the picture that we see is that contrary to expectations, the *uṣūl al-fiqh* and the *maqāṣid al-Sharīᶜah* have remained separate and the two have not been integrated to the extent needed to present a unified methodology and approach to the understanding of Sharīᶜah. For one thing, the *maqāṣid* represent a kind of a postscript or an afterthought, as it were, in the history of Islamic jurisprudence, which emerged centuries after the crystallisation of the legal theory of *uṣūl al-fiqh*. This might offer a partial explanation of why the *maqāṣid* has remained, to this day, on the margins of legal theory, and an undigested part that is not even included in the familiar presentations of the major themes of *uṣūl al-fiqh*. Many a reputable text of *uṣūl al-fiqh* does not even devote a chapter to the *maqāṣid al-Sharīᶜah* among the otherwise familiar range of its topics. This *lacuna* in the legal heritage is not accidental, partly because the *uṣūl* and the *maqāṣid*, when put side by side, can be seen as an uneasy combination. Conventional *uṣūl al-fiqh* is dominated by the literalist tradition, textual analysis and restrictive forms of interpretation. The *maqāṣid al-Sharīᶜah* is on the other hand dominantly goal-oriented and derives much of its substance from the broader perspective of reading the meaning and philosophy of the law through the words and lines of the text. The text and the goals of Sharīᶜah are to be read together in an integrated approach, and yet it is the higher objective of the law that commands priority in the event of technical obstacles which might separate one from the other.

Another notable difference between the *uṣūl* and the *maqāṣid* is the sheer amount of scholarly attention that the former has received through the centuries of scholastic developments and the rich literary heritage of Islamic law. The *uṣūl al-fiqh* is rich, one might even say too rich, and endowed with a distinctive methodology both generally and in its various component parts. The *maqāṣid al-Sharīᶜah*, on the other hand, presents us with a dynamic outlook on Sharīᶜah which is unfettered by technicality and yet somewhat lacking in methodological identity and substance. The *uṣūl* and the *maqāṣid* each have their strengths and weaknesses which might keep them apart in the absence of efforts that would help to bridge the gap between them. For they are essentially an extension of one another and any differences that might exist between them are basically concerned with externality and form.

There can be no denial of the unity of purpose between the *uṣūl* and the *maqāṣid* as indeed there are elements in both that can be utilised in the interests of the consolidation of the legal theory of Sharīᶜah, and *istiḥsān* can also be gainfully employed toward that end. Being an integral theme and topic of *uṣūl al-fiqh*, which is inherently generic and versatile, *istiḥsān* has equally strong grounds of identity with the *maqāṣid*. It should, in fact, be evident from our discussion of *istiḥsān* throughout this presentation that the evidential basis, rationale and purpose of *istiḥsān* are almost identical with those of the *maqāṣid al- Sharīᶜah*. *Istiḥsān* can thus be seen as an instrument of consolidation that can link up the major themes of the *uṣūl* and the *maqāṣid* into an organic unity. Our perusal of Islamic juristic thought shows on the other hand that the unifying potentials of *istiḥsān* have not been acknowledged in the scholastic treatment of principle.

The *uṣūlī* treatment of *istiḥsān* has been fraught with unwarranted controversy and although, for a brief moment, there was almost overwhelming acknowledgement of the inner riches of *istiḥsān* by Imam Mālik when he characterised it as 'nine-tenths of knowledge' this was soon followed by Imam al-Shāfiʿī's outright rejection of *istiḥsān*. If one were to characterise these contrasting positions, one would evidently strike a note with a pro-*maqāṣid* and the other with pro-literalist *uṣūlī* approach. *Istiḥsān* has been marginalised and its potential for bringing about unity between the Traditionist and Rationalist (Ahl al-Ḥadīth/ Ahl al-Ra'y) approaches to the understanding of Sharīʿah has been neither articulated nor internalised by the legal theory of *uṣūl al-fiqh*. Instead of seeing *istiḥsān* as an instrument of systematisation that could unify diverging strands in the juristic thoughts of the leading Imams, its weaknesses were emphasised, and the literalist tradition carried the moment.

Since *istiḥsān* is endowed with a methodology that looks in two directions: the textual proofs, *ijmāʿ*, *qiyās*, *maṣlaḥah* and custom on the one hand, and the goals and purposes of Sharīʿah on the other, and since it seeks to realise the ends of Sharīʿah through the evidential support of its means, it offers a unique methodology for synthesising the two undigested chapters of Islamic jurisprudential thought. The theory of *istiḥsān* is focused on finding a better alternative to a ruling or evidence of Sharīʿah when application of that ruling runs contrary to the *maqāṣid* of the same. There is a departure from an existing position to a preferable alternative when this is supported by one of the recognised proofs of *uṣūl al-fiqh*. In outline the formula that we have in *istiḥsān* is in many ways unique in that it combines the major themes of the *maqāṣid* with the methodological applications of *uṣūl*.

There should be no inherent contradiction in recognising both a primary and a secondary role for *istiḥsān* in its capacity as an instrument of convergence between the *uṣūl* and the *maqāṣid*. In its primary and normative capacity *istiḥsān* may be utilised to ensure harmony between the textual proofs and the *maqāṣid* by reference to alternative evidence in the textual proofs themselves. The emphasis here would be one of ensuring integrity and coherence between the text and the goal of Sharīʿah in that the one should not be read in isolation from the other. Should a conflict arise between these two aspects of the *aḥkām*, whether conceptual or in terms of application, *istiḥsān* could be utilised to vindicate the preferable reading of the text.

As for the methodology of *istiḥsān*, it has been stated that the potential for analogical *istiḥsān*, which involves abandoning an open analogy (*qiyās jalī*) for a hidden analogy (*qiyās khafī*) might be somewhat limited. This is because *qiyās* itself has almost exhausted its own potential, and this is attested by the fact that one hardly finds fresh examples of *qiyās* in the relevant literature of *fiqh*. To construct a second *qiyās* over an existing *qiyās* is a theoretically attractive proposition but one which can run into complexity and give rise to doubt. We leave open, of course, the possibility of recourse to analogical *istiḥsān*, which may be utilised as a corrective measure and an escape from the rigidity of an obvious *qiyās*. Exceptional *istiḥsān* would thus remain the chief stronghold of the methodology of *istiḥsān*. In the interest of methodological accuracy and caution in relation to *istiḥsān*, I have proposed that we should identify, as far as possible, the particular effective cause of *istiḥsān* whenever it is invoked in regard to particular issues. I have also argued in this connection that the identification of the *ᶜillah* need not be done in a highly technical manner—indeed, the exercise should be kept relatively non-technical. This I believe would be more apt for the utilisation of *istiḥsān* as an instrument serving the broader objectives or *maqāṣid* of the Sharīᶜah. Lastly, with reference to the varieties of *istiḥsān*, I have proposed adding two new varieties of exceptional *istiḥsān* that are founded on considerations of equity (*iḥsān*) and the removal of hardship (*rafᶜ al-ḥaraj*) respectively.

Glossary

ʿadl (also *ʿadala*): justice in general, and also uprightness of character in a witness.

aḥkām (pl. of *ḥukm*): a ruling of Sharīʿah, also a court judgement.

ahl al-ḥadīth: tradionists, chief advocates and partisans of ḥadīth.

ahl al-ḥall wa'l-ʿaqd: people who loosen and bind, persons in charge of community affairs.

ahl al-ra'y: rationalists, partisans of personal opinion.

amīn: trustee.

ʿamm: general, a general word or ruling that is not specified nor qualified.

ʿaqd: contract.

ʿāqila: agnatic relatives of the offender in criminal law.

ʿariyya: a barter exchange of unripe dates on the tree for dry dates.

ʿāriya: temporary loan of movable objects.

ʿaṣaba: agnatic relatives of the deceased in intestate succession.

bāṭil: null and void.

bayʿ: sale, contract of sale.

bayʿ bi-thaman ajil (also known as *bayʿ muʿajjal*): deferred payment sale.

bayʿ al-dayn bi'l-dayn: sale of debts, debt clearance sale.

bayʿ al-juzāf: a lump sum sale.

bayt al-māl: public treasury.

ḍamān: liability for loss.

dayn: deferred liability or obligation arising from a contract.

ḍarar: prejudice, harm.

ḍarūra: necessity that calls for relaxation of normal rules.

dhimma: personal responsibility and commitment.

fiqh: Islamic law, especially that part which is based on juristic opinion and construction.

faqīh: (pl. *fuqahā'*): jurist, one who is learned in *fiqh*.

fāsid: irregular, corrupt, but not totally devoid of legal consequences.

fatwā: (pl. *fatāwā*): juristic opinion, religious edict of a qualified jurist.
fuḍūlī: unauthorised person, uncommissioned agent.
ghabn: manipulation, fraud.
gharar: risk-taking and uncertainty in transactions and contracts.
gharar al-kathīr: excessive *gharar*.
gharar al-yasīr: minor *gharar*.
ḥabal al-habāl: sale of an unborn animal.
ḥabs: retention, holding, incarceration.
ḥadd: lit.limit, prescribed penalties in Islamic law.
ḥaqq: a right, entitlement.
ḥaraj: hardship.
ḥarām: totally forbidden.
ʿibādāt: (pl. of *ʿibāda*): devotional matters and rituals of worship.
ibāḥah: permissibility.
ijārah: a lease or hire contract.
ijmāʿ: consensus of scholars and jurists.
ijtihād: lit. exertion, independent reasoning by a qualified scholar to obtain legal rulings from the sources of Sharīʿah.
ʿillah: effective cause, or *ratio legis*, of a particular ruling.
istiṣnāʿ: contract of manufacture.
jihād: struggle for a worthy cause, including military struggle.
jumhūr: dominant majority.
juzāfan: as a lump sum.
khiyār: option.
khiyār al-sharṭ: option of cancellation in a contract .
liʿān: imprecation, a form of divorce in Islamic law.
madhhab: (pl. *madhāhib*): school of law or theology.
madrasah: traditional Islamic school.
maraḍ al-mawt: death illness.
maʿrūf: fair and just, also customary.
maṣlaḥah: public interest.
muʿāmalāt: (pl. of *muʿāmala*): a civil or commercial transaction (as opposed to *ʿibadat*).
muḍārabah: *commenda* contract, sleeping partnership.
muḍarib: the active partner in *muḍārabah*.
muftī: jurisconsult.
mujtahid: a competent jurist, one who is capable of conducting *ijtihād*.
murābaḥah: sale of something at cost plus profit.
mutʿah: gift of consolation in a divorce that takes place prior to consummation of marriage.
mutawallī: supervisor, especially of religious endowment or *waqf*.

nāfidh: effective.
naṣṣ (pl. *nuṣūṣ*): a clear text, esp. of the Qur'ān.
nikāḥ: marriage.
qabḍ: taking something into one's possession.
qāḍī: judge.
qarḍ: loan.
qarḍ ḥasan: a benevolent loan that does not carry interest.
qaṭʿī: definitive, decisive.
qiyās: analogy, analogical reasoning.
rabb al-māl: owner of capital, capital provider.
rafʿ al-ḥaraj: removal of hardship.
ra'y: a considered opinion.
ribā': usury.
ribā' al-faḍl: usurious excess in a sale that violates equivalence in countervalues.
ribā' al-nasi'a: credit based *ribā'*.
rukhṣah: concession, exemption.
safīh: an idiot, a person of impaired judgement.
salam: advance payment sale.
ṣarf: currency exchange.
Shiʿah: lit. faction, a minority *madhhab* of Islam.
sunnah: saying, teaching and exemplary conduct of the Prophet Muḥammad.
tabarruʿ: an act of charity and good will.
tābiʿūn: Successors, the generation following that of the Companions.
takhliya: evacuation.
takhṣīṣ: particularisation of the general.
taqlīd: indiscriminate imitation.
ummah: the Muslim community worldwide.
ʿurf: custom and usage of people.
uṣūl al-fiqh: science of the sources of law in Islam.
waḍīʿah: a deposit.
wakāla: agency.
wakīl: authorised agent, representative.
walī: guardian.
Ẓahirī: an extant school of Islamic law that inclined toward literalism.
ẓannī: speculative, open to interpretation.
ẓihār: a form of divorce in Islamic law.

Bibliography

Abū Dāwūd, *Sunan Abū Dāwūd*. Eng. trans. Aḥmad Ḥasan, 3 vols. Lahore: Ashraf Press, 1984.

Abū Sulaymān, ʿAbd al-Wahhāb Ibrāhīm, *Al-Fikr al-Uṣūli*, 2nd edn. Jeddah: Dār al-Sharq, 1404/1984.

Abū Yusuf, Yaʿqūb Ibrāhīm. *Kitāb al-Kharāj*. 2nd edn. Cairo: Al-Maṭbaʿah al-Salafiyyah, 1352 AH.

Abū Zahrah, Muḥammad. *Abū Ḥanīfah: Ḥayātuh wa ʿAṣruh, Arā'uh wa Fiqhuh*. Cairo: Dār al-Fikr al-ʿArabī, 1366/1947.

——. *Mālik: Ḥayātuh wa ʿAṣruh, Arā'uh wa Fiqhuh*. 2nd edn. Cairo: Dār al-Fikr al-ʿArabī, 1952.

——. 'Taʿliq ʿala Mawduʿ al-Istiḥsān wa'l-Maṣāliḥ al-Mursalah,' in *Al-Majlis al-Aʿla li-Riʿāyat al-Funun wa'l-Adab wa'l-ʿUlūm al Ijtimaʿiyyah, Usbuʿ al-Fiqh al-Islāmī wa Mihrajān al-Imām Ibn Taymiyyah*. Damascus: n.p., 1380/1960 AH.

——. *Uṣūl al-Fiqh*. Cairo: Dār al-Fikr al-ʿArabī, 1377/1958.

Al-Āmidī, Sayf al-Dīn. *Al-Iḥkām fī Uṣūl al-Aḥkām*. Ed. ʿAbd al-Razzāq ʿAfifi. Beirut: Al-Maktab al-Islāmī, 1402/1982.

Amin, Hassan ʿAbd Allah. 'Waqf in Islamic Jurisprudence' in *Management and Development of Awqaf Properties*. Jeddah: Islamic Research and Training Institute, 1407/1987.

——. 'Al-Waqf fi'l-Fiqh al-Islāmī,' in Hassan Amin (ed.), *Idārah wa Tathmīr Mumtalakāt al-Awqāf*, Al-Maʿhad al-Islāmī li'l-Buḥūth wa'l-Tadrīb. Jeddah, 1404/1984, 41–139.

Al-Andalusī, Muḥammad ʿAlī ibn Aḥmad ibn Hazm. *Al-Iḥkām fī Uṣūl al-Aḥkām*. Cairo: Maṭbaʿah al-Muniriyyah 1347 AH.

Attia, Gamal. 'Financial Instruments used by Islamic Banks,' in Butterworth Editorial Staff (ed.), *Islamic Banking and Finance*. London: Butterworths, 1986.

Bacha, Ubiyathulla Ismath. 'Conventional Versus Mudarabah Financing,' *Journal of Islamic Economics and Management* (International

Islamic University Malaysia) (Forthcoming).
Al-Bājī, Abū al-Walīd Sulaymān. *Al-Muntaqā Sharḥ al-Muwaṭṭā*. Beirut: Dār al-Kitāb al-ʿArabī, 1332 AH.
Al-Baʿlī, ʿAbd al-Ḥamīd Maḥmūd. *Asāsiyyāt al-ʿAmal al-Maṣrafī al-Islāmī: Al-Wāqiʿ wa'l-Āfāq*. Cairo: Maktabah Wahbah, 1410/1990.
Al-Bazdawī, Fakhr al-Islām ʿAlī ibn Muḥammad. *Uṣūl al-Bazdawī*, on the Margin of *Kashf al-Asrār*. Constantinople, 1307 AH.
Al-Bukhārī, Muḥammad ibn Ismāʿīl. *Ṣaḥīḥ al-Bukhārī*. Eng. Trans. Muḥammad Muḥsin Khān. Lahore: Kazi Publications, 1979.
Al-Farrā, Abū Yaʿlā Muḥammad ibn al-Ḥusayn. *Al-ʿUddah fī Uṣūl al-Fiqh*. Aḥmad ibn ʿAlī al-Mubārakī (ed.). Beirut: Mu'assasah al-Risālah, 1400/1980.
Gerber, Haim, 'Rigidity Versus Openness in Late Classical Islamic Law: The Case of the Seventeenth Century Palestinian Mufti Khayr al-Dīn al-Ramlī', in *Islamic Law and Society* 5, 2 (1998): 165–195.
Al-Ghazālī, Abū Ḥāmid Muḥammad. *Al-Mustaṣfa min ʿIlm al-Uṣūl*. Cairo: Al-Maktabah al-Tijāriyyah, 1356/1937.
Gieraths, Christine. 'Pakistan: Financial Products,' in R. Wilson (ed.), *Islamic Financial Markets*. London: Routledge, 1990.
Hamilton (see al-Marghinānī).
Ḥamoud, Sāmī Ḥasan. *Taṭwīr al-Aʿmal al-Maṣrafiyyah bi-ma Yattafiq wa al-Sharīʿah al-Islāmiyyah*, 2nd edn. Oman: Maṭbaʿah al-Sharq, 1402/1982.
Al-Harran, Saad (ed.). *Leading Issues in Islamic Banking and Finance*. Kuala Lumpur: Pelanduk Publications, 1995.
Ḥasan, Aḥmad. *Analogical Reasoning in Islamic Jurisprudence*. Islamabad: Islamic Research Institute, 1986.
——. 'The Principle of Istihsan in Islamic Jurisprudence', in *Islamic Studies*, 16 (1977), 347–363.
Hashmi, Sharafat Ali. 'Management of Waqf: Past and Present,' in Islamic Research and Training Institute, *Management and Development of Awqaf Properties*. Jeddah, 1407/1987, 19–27.
Al-Ḥusarī, Aḥmad. *Al-Dawlah wa Siyāsat al-Ḥukm fī'l-Fiqh al-Islāmī*. Vol. 2. Cairo: Maktabah al-Kulliyāt al-Azhariyyah, 1408/1988.
Ibn ʿĀbidin, Muḥammad Amīn. *Ḥāshiyah Radd al-Mukhtār ʿala Durr al-Mukhtār*. Cairo: Dār al-Fikr, 1399/1979.
Ibn al-Ḥājib, Jamāl al-Dīn Abū ʿAmr. *Mukhtaṣar al-Muntahā'*. Constantinople: al-Maktabah al-Islāmiyyah, 1310 AH.
Ibn al-Humām, Kamāl al-Dīn. *Fatḥ al-Qadīr Sharḥ al-Hidāyah*. Egypt: Būlāq, 1315–1318 AH.

Ibn Mājah, Muḥammad b. Yazīd al-Qazwīnī. *Sunan Ibn Mājah*. Istanbul: Cagri Yaginlari, 2 vols. 1401/1981.

Ibn al-Muqaffaᶜ, ᶜAbd Allāh. 'Risalah fil-Sahabah,' in Muḥammad Kurd Ali (ed.), *Risalat al-Bulagha*. 4th edn. Cairo, n.p., 1954.

Ibn Qayyim al-Jawziyyah. *Iᶜlām al-Muwaqqiᶜīn ᶜan Rabb al-ᶜĀlāmin*. Ed. Muḥammad Munīr al-Dimashqī. Cairo: Idārah al-Ṭībāᶜah al-Munīriyyah. 4 vols., n.d.

——. *al-Ṭuruq al-Ḥukmiyyah fi'l-Siyāsah al-Shariᶜiyyah*. Cairo: Mu'assasah al-ᶜArabiyyah li'l-Ṭībāᶜah, 1380/1961.

Ibn Qudāmah, see Al-Maqdisī.

Ibn Rushd al-Qurṭubī, Muḥammad b. Aḥmad . *Bidāyah al-Mujtahid*. Cairo: Muṣṭafā al-Bābī al-Ḥalabī, 1401/1981.

Ibn Taymiyyah, Taqī al-Dīn. 'Mas'alah al-Istiḥsān.' trans. and ed. George Makdisi as 'Ibn Taymiyyah's Manuscript on Istihsan,' in G. Makdisi (ed.), *Arabic and Islamic Studies in Honour of Hamilton A.R. Gibb*. Cambridge: Harvard University Press, 1965.

——. *Majmuᶜah Fatāwā Shaykh al-Islam Ibn Taymiyyah*. (ed.). Muḥammad Muhayy al-Dīn ᶜAbd al-Hamīd. Beirut: Dār al-Kutub, 1398/1978.

Ingram, Tim. 'Islamic Banking: A Foreign Bank's View,' in Butterworths Editorial Staff. *Islamic Banking and Finance*. London: Butterworths, 1986.

Islamic Research and Training Institute (IRTI) Seminar Proceedings, *Management and Development of Awqaf Properties*. Jeddah (Saudi Arabia), 1407/1987.

'Istihsan,' in *Mawsuᶜah al-Fiqh al-Islāmī*. Cairo: Dār al-Kitāb al-Miṣrī. Vol. 6, 27–47.

Al-Jassās, Aḥmad Ibn ᶜAlī al-Razī. *Uṣūl al-fiqh al-Musamma al-fusul fi'l-uṣūl*. Kuwait: n.p., 1985.

Al-Jīlānī, Abu'l-Qāsim b. Ḥasan. *Qawānīn al-Uṣūl*. Tehran: Dal al-Tababaᶜah Ali Qulikhan, 1299 AH.

Al-Jundī, Muḥammad. *Muᶜāmalāt al-Burṣah fi'l-Sharīᶜah al-Islāmiyyah*. Cairo: Dar al-Nahdah al-ᶜArabiyyah, 1409/1988.

Kamali, Mohammad Hashim, *Principles of Islamic Jurisprudence*, 2nd edn. Cambridge: Islamic Texts Society, 1991.

——. 'Have We Neglected the Shariᶜa Law Doctrine of Maslahah?' *Islamic Studies*. 33 (1988), 287–305.

Kassim, Husain, 'Sarakhsī's Doctrine of Juristic Preference (Istiḥsān) as a Methodological Approach towards Worldly Affairs (Aḥkām al-Dunyā)', *American Journal of Islamic Social Sciences*, 5 (1988), 181–205.

Kerr, Malcolm. *Islamic Reform*. Berkeley: University of California Press, 1961.

Khallāf, ʿAbd al-Wahhāb. *ʿIlm Uṣūl al-Fiqh*. 12th edn. Kuwait: Dār al-Qalam, 1398/1978.

al-Khuḍarī, Muḥammad. *Tā'rīkh al-Tashrīʿ al-Islāmī*. 7th edn. Beirut: Dār al-Fikr, 1401/1981.

——. *Uṣūl al-Fiqh*, 7th edition. Cairo: Dār al-Fikr.

Maḥmassānī, Subḥī. *Falsafah al-Tashrīʿ fi'l-Islām: The Philosophy of Jurisprudence in Islam*. Trans. Farhat J. Ziadeh. Leiden: E. J. Brill, 1961.

——. *Al-Mawjibāt wa'l-ʿUqūd fi'l-Sharīʿah al-Islāmiyyah*, 3rd edn. Beirut: Dār al-ʿIlm li'l-Malāyīn, 1983.

Makdisi, John, 'Legal Logic and Equity in Islamic Law'. *American Journal of Comparative Law*, 33 (1985), 63–92.

Al-Maqdisī, Ibn Qudāmah. *Al-Mughnī*. Riyad: Maktabah al-Riyāḍ al-Ḥadīthah, 1401/1981.

Al-Marghinānī, Burhān al-Dīn. *The Hidāya*. Eng. Trans. Charles Hamilton. Lahore: Premier Book House, 1975.

Al-Mashāt, Muḥammad ibn Ḥasan. *Al-Jawāhir al-Thamīnah*. Ed. ʿAbd al-Wahhāb Ibrāhīm Abū Sulaymān. Beirut: Dār al-Gharb al-Islāmī, 1406/1986.

Mawsūʿah al-Fiqh al-Islāmī. Cairo: Dār al-Kitāb al-Miṣrī, 1970.

Mikādi, Maḥmūd ʿAbd al-Qādir. 'Bahth fi'l-Istiḥsān' in *Al-Majlis al-Aʿla li-Riʿāyat al-Funun wa'l-Adab wa'l-ʿUlūm al-Ijtimaʿiyyah, Usbuʿ al-Fiqh al-Islāmī wa Mihrajān al-Imām Ibn Taymiyyah*. Damascus: n.p., 1380/1960, 297–343.

The Mejelle: Being An English Translation of Majallah al-Ahkam el-Adliya by C.R. Tyser. Lahore: Law Publishing Company, 1967.

Mīqā, Abū Bakr Ismāʿīl Muḥammad. *Al-Ra'y wa Atharuh fī Madrasah al-Madīnah*. Beirut: Mu'assasah al-Risālah, 1405/1985.

Mūsā, Muḥammad Yūsuf. *Al-Madkhal li-Dirāsah al-Fiqh al-Islāmī*. 2nd. edn. Cairo: Dār al-Fikr al-ʿArabī, 1373/1953.

Al-Nabhānī, Muḥammad Taqī al-Dīn. *Muqaddimah al-Dustūr*. Beirut: n.p., 1967.

Osborn, P.G. *A Concise Law Dictionary*. 5th edn. London: Sweet and Maxwell, 1964.

Al-Qarāfi, Shihāb al-Dīn. *Tabsirat al-Hukkām*. Ed. Tāha ʿAbd al-Raūf Saʿd. Cairo: Maktabah Kulliyyāt al-Azhariyyah, 1406/1986.

The Holy Qur'an, Text, Translation and Commentary by Abdullah Yusuf Ali. Jeddah: Islamic Education Centre, 1984.

Al-Qurṭubī, see Ibn Rushd.

Al-Ramlī, Khayr al-Dīn. *Fatāwā*. In the margins of Ibn Ḥajar al-Haytamī. al-Fatāwā al-Kubrā al-Fiqhiyya. 4 vols. Egypt: Būlāq, 1308 AH.

Al-Ṣābūnī, ʿAbd al-Raḥmān, *et al. Al-Madkhal al-Fiqhī wa Tārīkh al-Tashrīʿ al-Islāmī*. Cairo: Maktabah Wahbah, 1402/1982.

Ṣadr al-Sharīʿa, ʿUbayd Allah b. Masʿūd al-Mahbūbī. *Al-Tawḍīḥ fī Ḥall Ghawāmid al-Tanqīḥ*. Cairo: Dār al-ʿAhd al-Jadīd li'l-Tibaʿah, 1957.

Sahnūn, ʿAbd al-Salām Ibn Saʿīd. *Al-Mudawwanah al-Kubrā*. Cairo: Al-Maktabah al-Khayriyyah, 1324/1909.

Al-Sarakhsī, Shams al-Dīn Abū Bakr Muḥammad. *Al-Mabsūṭ*. Beirut: Dār al-Maʿrifah, 1406/1986.

——. *Uṣūl al-Sarakhsī*. Abu'l-Wafā al-Afghānī (ed.). Cairo: Maṭbaʿah Dār al-Kitāb al-ʿArabī, 1372 AH.

Shaʿbān, Zakī al-Dīn. *Uṣūl al-Fiqh al-Islāmī*. Kuwait: Jāmiʿah al-Kuwait, n.d.

Al-Shāfiʿī, Muḥammad b. Idrīs. *Kitāb al-Umm*. Cairo: Dār al-Shaʿb, 1321 AH.

——. *Al-Risālah*. Ed. Muḥammad Sayyid Kīlānī, 2nd edn. Cairo: Muṣṭafā al-Bābī al-Ḥalabī, 1403/1983.

Al-Shāṭibī, Abū Isḥāq Ibrāhīm, *al-Muwāfaqāt fī Uṣūl al-Sharīʿʾah*. Ed. Shaykh ʿAbd Allāh Dirāz. Cairo: al-Maktabah al-Tijāriyyah al-Kubrā, n.d.

——. *al-Iʿtiṣām*. Cairo: Maṭbaʿah al-Manār, 1331/1914.

al-Shawkānī, Yaḥyā b. ʿAlī, *Irshād al-Fuhūl min Taḥqīq al-Ḥaqq ilā ʿIlm al-Uṣūl*. Cairo: Dār al-Fikhr, n.d.

——. *Nayl al-Awṭār Sharḥ Muntaqā al-Akhbār*. Cairo: Muṣṭafā al-Bābī al-Ḥalabī, n.d.

Al-Shaybānī, Muḥammad b. Ḥasan. *Al-Siyar al-Kabīr*. Hyderabad: n.p., 1335 AH.

——. *Al-Aṣl*. Cairo, n.p., 1966–1973.

Siddiqui, Muḥammad Nejatullah. *Banking Without Interest*. Lahore: Islamic Publications Ltd., reprint 1991.

Simawnah, Badr al-Dīn Maḥmūd ibn Isrā'īl Ibn Qādi. *Jāmiʿ al-Fusulayn*. Cairo: Maṭbaʿah al-Amiriyyah, 1300 AH.

Al-Subkī, Tāj al-Dīn. *Jamʿ al-Jawāmiʿ fī'l-Uṣūl*. 2nd edn. Cairo: Muṣṭafā al-Bābī al-Ḥalabī, 1365 AH.

Sum, Wong Choo. 'Bank Islam Malaysia: Performance Evaluation 1983–1993,' in Harran (ed.). *Islamic Banking*, 83–103.

Al-Taftāzānī, Saʿd al-Dīn Masʿūd. *Sharḥ al-Talwīḥ ʿala'l-Tawḍīḥ*. Beirut: Dār al-Kutub al-ʿIlmiyyah, n.d.

ᶜUmar al-Dīn, Muḥammad. 'Istiḥsān and Masalih-e Mursalah,' in *Al-Majlis al-Aᶜla li-Riᶜāyat al-Funun wa'l-Adab wa'l-ᶜUlūm al-Ijtimaᶜiyyah, Usbuᶜ al-Fiqh al-Islāmī wa Mihrajān al-Imām Ibn Taymiyyah.* Damascus: n.p., 1380/1960, 347–355.

Wehr, Hans. *Arabic-English Dictionary.* Ed. J.M. Cowan. New York: Spoken Language Service Inc., 1976.

Wilson, Rodney, (ed.). *Islamic Financial Markets.* London: Routledge, 1990.

——. 'Islamic Development Finance in Malaysia,' in Harran (ed.). *Islamic Banking,* 59–83.

Yusuf, Ridwan Aremu. 'The Theory of Istihsan (Juristic Preference) in Islamic Law,' unpublished Ph.D Dissertation, Montreal: McGill University, 1993.

Al-Zarqa, Anas. 'Some Modern Means for the Financing and Investment of Awqaf Projects,' in Islamic Research and Training Institute, *Management and Development of Awqaf Properties.* Jeddah, 1407/1987, 38–49.

Al-Zarqā, Muṣṭafā Aḥmad. *Al-Madkhal al-Fiqhī al-ᶜĀmm.* 6th edn. Damascus: Dār al-Fikr, 1967.

——. *Sharḥ al-Qawāᶜid al-Fiqhiyyah.* 3rd edn. Damascus: Dār al-Qalam, 1414/1993.

——. *Al-Istiṣlāḥ wa Masālih al-Mursalah fī'l-Sharīᶜah al-Islāmiyyah.* Damascus: Dār al-Qalam, 1408/1988.

Zaydān, ᶜAbd al-Karīm. *Al-Wajīz fī Uṣūl al-Fiqh.* Baghdad: Maktabah al-Quds, 1396/1976.

Al-Zaylaᶜī, ᶜUthmān bin ᶜAlī. *Tabyīn al-Ḥaqā'iq Sharḥ Kanz al-Daqā'iq.* Egypt: Būlāq, 1313 AH.

Al-Zuḥaylī, Wahbah. *Uṣūl al-Fiqh al-Islāmī.* Damascus: Dār al-Fikr li'l-Ṭibāᶜah wa'l-Tawziᶜ wa'l-Nashr, 1406/1986.

Index

^{c}Abduh, Muḥammad, 122
Abū Ḥanīfah, 13,17, 18, 21, 32, 37, 40, 44, 66, 71, 72, 76, 95, 96
Abū Yūsuf, 19, 20, 33, 37, 40, 69
Abū Zahrah, 20, 65, 67
^{c}*adl*, 55
al-Afghānī, 122
agricultural states, 93
aḥabbu ilayya, 20
al-aḥkām, 3,4,121,125
Ahl al-Ḥadīth, 18, 66, 120, 121, 124
ahl al-hall wa'l-^{c}*aqd*, 44
Ahl al-Kitāb, 38
aḥsan, 60
al-ajīr al-mushtarak, 39, 40
al-ajīr al-khāṣṣ, 40
al-ajīr al-^{c}*āmm*, 40
^{c}Alī ibn Abī Ṭālib, 24, 44, 45, 118
al-alwāḥ, 58
al-Āmidī, 22, 25, 44, 61, 78
amīn (trustee), 20, 39, 109, 115
^{c}*āmm*, 36
analogy, see *qiyās*
^{c}*aqd jā'iz*, 96
^{c}*āqilah*, 20
^{c}*aql* (rationality), see *al-shar*^{c} *aw al-*^{c}*aql*
aqwa al-dalilayn, 13
Arabic language, 89, 121
^{c}*arāyā* (sale), 60
^{c}*āriyah*, 96
^{c}*ariyyah*, 27
arfaq, 24
^{c}*aṣabah*, 44
Asbagh ibn Faraj ibn Sa^{c}īd al-Mālikī, 21
al-aṣl fi'l-dīn, 25
assets, 97, 98, 107, 116
  muḍārabah assets, 104
astaḥsinu, 20
  astaḥsinu kadhā, 65
  astaḥsinu dhālika, 65
athar, 18
Attia, Gamal, 110
awqāf, 83, 92ff, 119
  awqāf khayriyyah, 99
  awqāf ahliyyah, 99

Bangladesh, 93
banking transactions, 40, 101, 102
al-Baṣrī, Abū'l-Ḥusayn, 12, 72
bay^{c} *al-mu'ajjal*, 102, 110
bay^{c} *bi-thaman ājil*, 102, 103, 110
al-bayt, 43
bayt al-māl, 118
bid^{c}*a*, 53
  bid^{c}*a mubāḥa*, 53
  bid^{c}*a mustaḥsanah*, 53
  bid^{c}*a qabīḥa*, 53
bi'l-ma^{c}*rūf*, 59
buyu^{c} *al-ājāl*, 43

charitable foundation, 119
Chechata, Chafik, 9
children, 59
Companions of the Prophet, ix, 6, 12, 13, 17, 33, 44, 55, 60, 61, 64, 79, 118
contract of sale, 83, 89
court, 96, 97, 114
  higher courts, 77, 97
  lower courts, 77
  supreme court, 97
custom, see *ᶜurf*

al-dayn al-mushtarak, 30
dalīl, 12, 18, 49, 59
  al-dalīl al-ᶜām, 72
ḍamān, 20, 39, 89, 111, 112
al-ḍararu yuzāl, 94
ḍarūrah, 12, 29, 36, 49, 51, 55
delivery, 86-88, 90
dhawū al-furūḍ, 44
dhimmah, 31
divorce, 64
diyyah, 20
dower and inheritance, 47, 48, 85, 89, 95

Egypt, 93, 99, 102, 104
Egyptian law, 41, 44
equity, see *istiḥsān*

FAO, 93
fāsid, 42
Faṣl fī Bayān Fasād al-Qawl bi-Jawāz al-Takhṣīṣ fī'l ᶜIlal al-Sharᶜiyyah, 73
fa'staḥsinū, 18
Fatāwā al-Khayriyya, 39
fatwā, 6, 38, 41, 63, 86
fī ḥūkm al-ᶜadam, 46
fiqh, x, 7, 29, 37, 42, 50, 53, 67, 76, 85, 87, 92–94, 96, 104, 105, 107, 112, 115, 122, 125
  fiqh of muḍārabah 104

al-fuḍūlī, 36, 46
  bona fide fuḍūlī, 46
food grains, 89, 90

al-ghabn al-yasīr, 46
gharar, 43, 47, 86, 87, 90, 91, 113
ghāsib, 68, 69
al-Ghazālī, al-Imām, 12, 51, 52, 61, 78
Gieraths, Christine, 110
gift, 45, 85, 89,
goods, 85, 103, 104, 109–111
  categories of goods, 85
    commodities, 33, 85–87, 89, 91
    foodstuffs, 85, 86, 89
  perishable goods, 86, 98
  types of goods, 85, 89
    immovable, 85, 90, 98
    movable, 85, 97, 98

ḥabs, 89
ḥadd, 5
ḥadīth, 19, 21, 24, 33, 34, 60, 61, 85, 86, 90, 94
Ḥakīm Ibn Ḥizām, 33
ḥammāl al-ṭaᶜām, 40
Ḥanafī *fiqh*, ix, 5, 12, 13, 21, 22, 26, 30, 32, 34, 36, 38ff, 45, 47–9, 58, 61, 63, 64, 66, 67, 73, 77, 79, 97
Ḥanafī and Mālikī, 49ff, 54
Ḥanbalī *fiqh*, ix, 5, 13, 22, 61, 63, 88, 90
ḥaqq al-masīl, 30
ḥaqq al-murūr, 30
ḥaqq al-shurb, 30, 42
ḥasana, 11
hawā, 66
Hidāyah, 58
higher courts, 77
al-Ḥimāriyyah, 44
al-ḥirz, 89
hospitals, 95

ḥujjiyyah, 58
ḥukm, x, 29, 59, 67, 71–73, 77

ᶜibādāt, 3, 27, 53, 121
Ibn ᶜAbbās, 44, 86
Ibn ᶜĀbidīn, 36
Ibn al-ᶜArabī, 13–15, 71
Ibn al-Ḥājib, 12, 22, 26, 48, 49
Ibn Ḥanbal, 21, 22, 44
Ibn Ḥazm al-Ẓāhirī, 66, 67, 89
Ibn Masᶜūd, ᶜAbd Allāh ibn, 44, 60, 66
Ibn al-Muqaffaᶜ, 19
Ibn al-Musayyib, Saᶜīd, 118
Ibn Qayyim al-Jawziyyah, 37, 38, 88
Ibn Qudāmah al-Maqdisī, 13, 22, 88, 89
Ibn Rushd, 21, 25, 50
Ibn Taymiyyah, 21, 38, 65, 72, 88, 89
Ibn ᶜUmar, 85, 86
al-ibrā, 32
al-idāᶜ, 32
īfā' al-dayn, 32
iḥsān, 4, 44, 54, 55, 76, 125
ijārah (lease), 30, 51, 69, 101, 103
ijmāᶜ, ix, 3, 7, 13, 25, 29, 44, 51, 52, 61, 66, 67, 75, 77, 78, 122, 124
ijtihād, 4, 5, 7, 12–4, 32, 59, 61, 63, 68, 75, 76, 94, 121, 122
Malikī *ijtihād*, 26
ᶜilal, 50
ᶜillah, x, 7, 15, 71–4, 76, 78–80, 87, 91, 96, 100, 106, 108, 109, 112, 125
Imāma, 48
Imāma al-mafḍūl, 48
Imāmī Shīᶜah, 67
Imāmiyyah, 67
imprecation, see *liᶜān*
inheritance, 34
  see dower and inheritance
intifāᶜ, 30
Iran, 102
Islamic banking, 83, 90, 101ff, 122
  transactions in, 101, 113
Islamic jurisprudence, 77, 83, 120
Islamic law, 38, 83, 102, 123
istaḥsanū, 66
istaqbahū, 66
al-istidlāl al-mursal, 21, 25, 65, 109, 121
al-istīfā', 32
istiḥbāb, 64
istiḥsān
  analogical *istiḥsān*, 75, 77–79, 125
  equity-based *istiḥsān*, 55, 79, 125
  exceptional *istiḥsān*, 75, 80, 125
  Ḥanafī *istiḥsān*, 65, 78
  istiḥsān and equity, ix, 8, 9, 54
  istiḥsān and *ijmāᶜ*, 35
  istiḥsān and *istiṣlāḥ*, 39
  istiḥsān and necessity *(ḍarūrah)*, 36, 49, 53
  istiḥsān ᶜal-aql, 53
  istiḥsān bi-murāᶜāt khilāf al-ᶜulamā, 44
  istiḥsān bi'l-naṣṣ, 33ff, 48, 69, 78
  istiḥsān bi-tark al-yasīr, 46
  istiḥsān al-faqīh, 52
  istiḥsān istithnā'ī, 8, 29
  istiḥsān maqbūl, 48
  istiḥsān mardūd, 48
  istiḥsan mutaradad, 48
  istiḥsān qiyāsī, 8, 29, 48, 67
  istiḥsān al-Shāriᶜ, 52
  istiḥsān al-Sunnah, 34
  Mālikī *istiḥsān*, 65
  maṣlaḥah based *istiḥsān*, 39, 41, 88, 105, 118
istiṣnāᶜ, 19, 35, 36, 90
istiṣlāḥ, 13, 39, 50, 68
Iyās b. Muᶜāwiyah, 17

*al-jam*ᶜ, 27
al-Jaṣṣāṣ, Abū Bakr, 12, 59
jumhūr, 97, 98
jurist, 4, 5, 7, 11, 48, 52, 59, 75-7, 107
later-day jurists (*muta'akhkhirūn*), 53, 68

al-Karkhī, Abū'l-Ḥasan, 11,12,14
Khālid Ibn al-Walīd, 69
Khayr al-Dīn al-Ramlī, 39, 53
al-khiyār, 25, 26
khiyār al-sharṭ, 26, 34, 35
al-Khuḍarī, 6
Kitāb al-Umm, 23, 63
Kitāb Ibṭal al-Istiḥsān, 63
kitābiyahs, 5

lawgiver, 52
law-letter and spirit of the law, 3, 76
lease, see *ijārah*
*li*ᶜ*ān*, 64
literal meaning, 6, 11
literalists, 120
literalist tradition, 123, 124
lower courts, 77

*ma'ālāt al-af*ᶜ*āl*, 15
ma'ālāt al-aḥkām, 72
madīnah, 19
madhāhib, 8, 61, 63, 95, 121
madrasahs, 95
mafsada, 26
Maḥmassānī, 12
Makdisi, John, 9
Malaysia, 87, 88, 102, 104, 118
Mālik ibn Anas, 13, 20, 21, 40, 43, 44, 47, 48, 65, 66, 71, 72, 124
Mālikī *fiqh*, ix, 5, 13, 15, 22, 25, 26, 40, 44, 46–48, 61, 63, 64, 66, 71, 77, 79, 90
al-maqāsah, 46
maqāṣid, x, 120–5
maraḍ al-mawt, 19, 20
marriage (*nikāḥ*), 37, 47, 48, 51
marjūh, 47
*marfū*ᶜ, 60
mark-up, 103, 104, 108–111
*mas'alat al-musta*ᶜ*ār li'l-rahn*, 46
al-maṣāliḥ al-mursalah, 64
masjid (mosque), 43, 95, 37
maṣlaḥah, ix, 3, 4, 7, 13, 15, 20, 24ff, 39ff, 49, 50, 52, 54, 61, 65, 72, 76, 79, 87, 100, 108, 109, 112, 116, 124
  maṣlaḥah juz'iyyah, 13, 21, 71
Medina, 38
Mīqā, Abū Bakr, 22
mismanagement, 92, 95, 97, 106
mortgage, 31-33, 46, 95, 104
Muᶜadh ibn Jabal, 24
*mu*ᶜ*āmalāt*, ix, 3, 4, 29, 121
muḍārabah, 22, 27, 83, 101ff
  muḍārabah assets, 104
  muḍārabah and mark-up, 108
  shibh al-muḍārabah, 106, 107
muḍārib, 22, 104-9
muftī, 64
mujtahid, 4, 7, 8, 11–14, 33, 48, 49, 53, 59, 67, 68, 72, 75–9, 122
mujtahidūn, 75
al-mukātab, 64
murābaḥah, 83, 101ff
murtadad, 49
musāqāt, 27
al-mushāhadah, 89
mushārakah, 83, 101ff, 108, 111ff
al-mushtarakah, 17, 44, 55, 64, 79
Muslims and non-Muslims, 19, 37, 38, 93, 102
mustahsinūn, 67
muta'akhkhirūn, 53
*mut*ᶜ*ah*, 59, 64
mutawalī, 95–97
Muᶜtazilah, 63, 73
*muzāra*ᶜ*ah*, 39

naṣṣ (explicit text), 7, 29, 63, 64
necessity, see *ḍarūrah*
non-Muslims, 19, 37, 38
nuṣūṣ, 7, 15

oaths, 50, 51
objectives of the *Sharīʿah*, see *maqāṣid*
OIC, 99
oral testimony, 7
orphanages, 119
Ottoman Turkey, 53

Pakistan, 93, 102, 104, 105, 110, 114
Paret, R., 9
paternity, 37
pension funds, 118, 119
positive law, ix
private property, 38, 41, 46, 94
profit, 106, 108, 110–115
Prophet, 6, 18, 24, 33, 38, 47, 51, 63, 64, 69, 85, 86
public bath, 42
purchase, 85, 89, 108, 109, 115

qabḍ, 83, 85ff
qāḍī, 95
Qādi Abū Yaʿlā al-Farrā, 21
qalaʿah, 19
al-Qarāfī, Shihāb al-Dīn, 18
al-qarā'in, 52
  al-qarā'in al-qānūniyyah, 52
  al-qarā'in al-qaḍā'iyyah, 52
qard, 27
  qard ḥasan, 27, 102
al-qayḍ al-ḥisābī, 90
qiyās (analogy), ix, 3–5, 7, 9, 12–5, 17–21, 25–7, 29, 32–5, 40, 48, 49, 51, 52, 59, 61, 64, 69, 71, 73, 75, 80, 98, 109, 119, 122, 124, 125
  qiyās jalī, 7, 8, 15, 29–33, 75, 76, 78, 125
  qiyās khafī, 7, 8, 22, 30, 32, 33, 49, 50, 75, 76, 78, 125
  qiyās mustaḥsan, 78
  qiyās sharʿī, 77
  al-qiyās al-ẓāhir, 32, 50
  irregularities and rigidities of *qiyās*, 49
  text-based *qiyās*, 77
Qur'ān, x, 3, 5, 6, 9, 12, 19, 24, 26, 33, 34, 43, 45, 51, 52, 55, 58-61, 63, 72, 75, 78–80, 94, 120, 122

rabb al-māl, 104, 106-8
Rāfiʿ Ibn Khadīj, 22
rafʿ al-ḥaraj, 5, 25, 26, 43, 44ff, 49, 54, 55, 125
rājih, 47
Ramadan, 60
rationality, see *al-sharʿ aw al- ʿaql*
Ahl al-Ra'y (Rationalists), 66, 120, 121, 124
ra'y, 6, 43, 59, 61, 68, 75, 76, 84, 121
ribā, 27, 43, 46, 47, 60, 111–113
  ribā al-nasi'ah, 113
  ribā-free transactions or banking, 101, 106
al-rifq, 24
al-Risāla, 23, 63
risk-sharing partnership, 113–6
riwāyah, 18

Ṣadr al-Sharīʿa al-Bukhārī, 73
ṣalāh, 27
salam contracts, 33, 34, 69, 90
sale, 83, 85–88, 90, 95, 96, 108, 109, 111, 112, 115
Ṣāliḥ Ibn Ḥanbal, 21
al-samāsirah al-mushtarakīn, 40
sanad, 61
al-Sarakhsī, Shams al-Dīn, 5, 12, 15, 24, 25, 59, 65, 68, 73, 74

ṣarīḥ locutions,
Schacht, J., 9
scripless trading, 85, 87, 88
al-Shāfiʿī, 22, 23, 44, 63–6, 68, 76, 86, 121, 124
Shāfiʿī *fiqh*, 5, 39, 51, 63, 64, 90
  pre-Shāfiʿī, 18
al-sharʿ aw al- ʿaql, 52
share, 93, 113, 114
  share certificates, 87, 88
  see also stocks
sharʿī evidence, 84, 121
Sharīʿah, x, 3-6, 8, 9, 13, 14, 18, 19, 21, 26, 27, 34, 50, 51, 53, 59–61, 65, 67, 71, 76, 87, 89, 93, 94, 102, 122, 124
  and natural law, 8
  maqāṣid al-sharīʿah, x, 120–123
al-Shāṭibī, Abū Isḥāq, 12, 13, 15, 25–27, 35, 47, 52, 53, 72, 120
al-Shawkānī, 14
al-Shaybānī, 17–19, 32, 36, 37, 40, 42, 68
Shīʿah, 63
Shīʿī *ʿulamā'*, 5
specification, see *takhṣīṣ*,
stocks, 98
  stocks and shares, 85, 87, 88, 98
al-Subkī, Tāj al-Dīn, 25
Successors (*tābiʿūn*), 6, 118
Sunnah, x, 3, 4, 6, 9, 12, 19, 21,22, 26, 33, 34, 42, 47, 51, 60, 61, 63, 72, 75, 78, 80, 94, 120, 122
  tacitly approved (*taqrīrī*) Sunnah, 51
Syria, 93, 99
  Syrian legislation, 44

tabarruʿ, 45, 46
tābiʿūn, see Successors
al-tafarruq, 89
al-Taftāzānī, 12
taḥāluf, 51
takhliyah, 89
takhṣīṣ, 71ff
  takhṣīṣ al-ʿumūm, 71
  takhṣīṣ al-qiyās, 71
  takhṣīṣ al-ʿillah, 72, 73
taladhudh wa-hawā, 23, 63
al-tanāqud, 73
al-taqādum, 52
taqlīd, 4
  anti-*taqlīd*, 121
al-tarakhkhusāt, 27
Tradition, 61
  Traditionists, 66
transactions, see Islamic banking
al-Ṭūfī, Najm al-Dīn, 22
Turkey, 93
Tyan, Emile, 9

ʿulamā, ix, 3, 8, 11, 12, 35, 44, 47, 54, 75, 78, 79, 85, 86, 121
ultra vires, 32, 34, 64, 69
ʿUmar ibn al-Khaṭṭāb, 5, 6, 17, 44, 45, 79, 118, 119
ummah, 25, 94
UNICEF, 93
ʿuqūd muʿāwadāt al-māliyyah, 42
ʿurf, 7, 13, 25ff, 29, 35, 36, 41ff, 48, 51, 67, 79, 85, 87–90, 97, 121, 124
usufruct, see *intifāʿ*
uṣūl al-fiqh, x, 3, 4, 5, 14, 17, 61, 75, 77, 109, 120-124
uṣūlī thought, 66
usury, see *ribā*
ʿUthmān ibn ʿAffān, 44, 61, 118, 119

al-waḍīʿah, 31, 32, 36, 40
wakālah, 45, 115
  wakālah khāṣṣah, 45
wakīl, 31, 45, 109, 115

waqf, x, 29, 37, 39–41, 92ff
waqīf, 41, 95, 98, 100
Western commentators, 9
Western law, 9, 54
WHO, 93
wilāyah, 37

Yusuf Ali, 59

ẓāhir al-riwāya, 39
Ẓahirī *fiqh*, 5, 63, 120
Zakī al-Dīn Shaʿbān, 33
ẓannī, 61, 62, 75
al-Zarqā, Muṣṭafā, 25, 50, 52, 67, 68, 93
Zayd ibn Thābit, 44
ẓihār, 64
Zufar ibn al-Hudhayl, 33